Nothing
So
Strange

The Autobiography of
Arthur Ford

in collaboration with
Margueritte Harmon Bro

Nothing
So
Strange

HARPER & ROW
Publishers NEW YORK

Contents

CHAPTER 1

Nothing So Strange

THERE IS NOTHING so strange as the way the strangeness
wears off the strange. Experiences that now seem commonplace once shook me to the depths. Some people are introduced gradually to the subject of psychic phenomena but
my introduction came as a bolt. One day I was a self-assured
young officer at Camp Grant, having recently arrived from
Fort Sheridan where I had become one of the ninety-day
wonders of World War I, a second lieutenant, and the next
day I was a mighty frightened boy in a different world.
Not because of the war, either, but because of a dream. Or
was it a dream?

That morning I had wakened from a night's sound sleep
with the roster of the names of those who had died of influenza in the night plain before my eyes. I thought my
experience must be the hang-over of a dream. I told myself
that when I got a look at the real roster, which it was my
duty to pick up from the adjutant's office, I would know I
had just imagined what I had just seen. But when I picked
up the list it was the same; not only the names were the ones
I had seen but they were in the exact order I had seen them.

I tried to shake off the experience.

But the next morning the same thing happened. As I

wakened, there was the list of fatalities. And again it checked out. Those were the days of the influenza epidemic and Camp Grant was hard hit. At one time I was the only officer in my company who was not down. Every morning at reveille men who had just been called from their beds were dropping to the ground; at night more men died in the hospital. Across the United States over half a million people died of flu. Everyone seemed under tension but mine was different—and worse.

The third morning I mentioned these strange goings-on to a couple of my buddies. They said, "You're kidding." I said I wished I were. So the next morning when we first wakened I told them the names that would appear that day. Sure enough, those names were posted. They said, "You're pulling some kind of a trick." I started to remonstrate but caught the look in their eyes, so I just laughed. "You figure it out," I said to them cockily. But I did not feel cocky and I could not figure it out.

I had never heard of precognition; I had never heard of clairvoyance; I did not know that the mind had an extrasensory reach. And if I had heard of such matters I would have thought that the person who told me was as crazy as the queer ducks he was talking about. In Titusville, Florida, where I grew up, the word *psychic* meant spirits and good Baptist boys had no truck with spirits. Ordinary people sometimes talked about fortune-tellers and water diviners and sometimes repeated ghost stories they had heard from servants or from someone who knew a man who knew a man who said . . . Premonitions of death were vaguely considered a mark of spirituality. And there our parapsychology ended.

After a week of this dream business I wanted to go to the chaplain or the doctor but I was afraid I might be sent to a mental hospital. Surely this strange disclosure of facts, which I could not know but did, would shut itself off as suddenly as it had come upon me. But instead of stopping, it took a different quirk. One morning I realized that the names I was seeing were no longer the names of flu victims but of men killed at the front. I would write down the names seen on waking and then check the casualty lists in the newspapers. Daily as new recruits moved in our men were being sent overseas; we were replacements for the Rainbow Division. Sometimes that very day, sometimes the next day, but always within a week, the names I had seen would appear in the newspaper and in the same order. Along with my persistent feeling of being strange I now became curious. Why did I get certain names, certain sections of a list, and not others? None of the names was known to me personally.

Finally I went to the Protestant chaplain. If he had met me with a strait jacket I would scarcely have been surprised. What he did was to listen to my story and then tell me to pray that God would take away these silly dreams. Dreams? Delusions? As though naming a process could control it, let alone stop it. And with about 85 per cent of my current "dreams" verifiable.

Finally I wrote to my mother to ask if there were any history of insanity in the family, not mentioning my reason for asking. She replied that there certainly was no insanity; she would like me to know I had some very smart forebears. But there was an aunt on my father's side of the family who was somewhat unbalanced. She was pleasant and harmless, my mother said, and the family had never made any move to commit her to an institution. So that explained Aunt Mary in Jacksonville. I had always realized there was something wrong with Aunt Mary because she was never discussed as the other members of the family were. Much later I found that Aunt Mary was a medium!

In the Baptist annals of those days a medium was definitely unmentionable.

My unbidden knowledge continued. In a way, what I knew was less upsetting than the method of knowing. According to the teaching that had come my way, all knowledge was derived from sense data which reached the brain through the approved channels of the five senses. To be sure, I believed—more or less—that Jesus had had a gift of foreknowledge but I took it for granted that such power, like the ability to heal the sick without medicine, was a direct gift from God and that the Son had passed it on only to his Twelve Apostles. The reports of any miracles that happened after the Bible went to print were mistakenly construed.

My most startling experience came the morning of the false armistice. I wakened with an acute feeling of depression, a deep misery not in keeping with my nature. When the announcement of peace came and people responded with hysterical joy, I knew the report was false.

The morning of the real Armistice was marked by my first flash of clairvoyant knowledge which had personal significance. As I opened my eyes I was startled to see the face of my brother George who was located at a southern army camp. He was smiling but I felt a sense of apprehension. Later I found that during the night he had come down with a severe case of influenza, soon augmented by complications from which he later died.

The next month I was given the choice of going to Russia or returning to school. I went back to Transylvania University at Lexington, Kentucky. In my day the faculty included a handful of real scholars. I still remember the intellectual excitement they afforded a Florida Cracker.

Back in the familiar round of classes my psychic miseries died down, but my anxiety nagged on, and in that fall of

1919 I elected a course in psychology. It was taught by Professor Elmer Snoddy, a big man of fine intelligence and ample academic background with a liberal theological point of view at a time when liberalism was fighting for a toehold. Our textbook was written by William McDougall of Harvard, then probably America's outstanding psychologist. One day in the course of a lecture on abnormal psychology Professor Snoddy made reference to the mind's extraordinary ability to acquire knowledge, at times, in ways outside the usual sensory channels. He documented a variety of psychic experience vouched for by as authentic an observer as William James. So I was not alone! But Snoddy presented his material objectively without comment as to what he thought about the subject. After class I pondered the matter. If I told him that I also found knowledge entering through the backdoor of my mind, so to speak, he might conclude that I was a queer one. At the same time, I wanted to talk with him too much to pass by this opening. I made an appointment and broached my problem.

Professor Snoddy was an eager listener and before I left his office he told me about the British and American Societies for Psychical Research. Serious men were seriously interested in the kind of non-sensory perception that had troubled me! I left Snoddy with William James' *Varieties of Religious Experience* in my hand. Also with an urgent invitation to come to his house and talk further.

We had many wonderful evenings. I know now how fortunate I was to have fallen into the hands of a man of his stature. He thought clearly, he was well-schooled, and he had great integrity. He wanted to know all about my background, and not just an outline of facts but the experiences that colored my thinking. This was certainly my first self-conscious attempt to see myself.

CHAPTER 2

From Jail to College

I WAS BORN in Titusville, Florida, population three hundred. All the town knew that my mother, Henrietta Brown Ford, had come home to have a second baby, bringing her two-year-old daughter, Annie, with her. My parents lived down at Fort Pierce, but my father was captain of a steamboat—a sturdy side-wheeler—which ran some two hundred miles of the Indian River's course from Daytona to Palm Beach, and it seemed better for my mother to go to her old home where her mother could help in her care. Families, in terms of three generations, were closer knit in those days.

My mother was a beautiful woman. This is the report of all who knew her. She was lithe and lovely, with dark hair and deep blue eyes. In fact, in 1925, when she was around fifty, she inadvertently won a beauty contest in Miami as the most beautiful woman of her age group.

My father was tall and fine looking. His name was Albert Fordeaux, but I never knew about the *eaux* or the French descent until I was out of college and living in New York when a psychic gave me a tip on the family. As a child all I knew about my father's family was that my grandfather had also been named Albert Ford and that when my father was five my grandfather had gone to New York by sailing

6

vessel to visit relatives, that the vessel was wrecked in a storm and that he was reported among those drowned. So my grandmother moved to the central part of Florida, a pioneering venture in those days before railroads, and reared her two children—my father and his stepsister. This stepsister of his, my Aunt Florence Prevatt, told me stories of the family "back in Carolina" in the slaveholding days. My father knew that he had relatives in the North but he never tried to locate them. In those days the North was very far away, both psychologically and in point of mileage.

I was born in jail.

My grandfather Brown was deputy sheriff and in those days it was customary for the sheriff to live in the commodious county building which also housed the jail. It was a pleasant place with a huge lawn spread under live oak trees. But that January 8 was a cold gray day, I'm told, and my mother made a fine hot ragout for the family before she called the doctor.

When I was three weeks old my mother dressed her plump young son in his best—the dress four times as long as the baby and intricately tucked and belaced—and took the side-wheeler back to Fort Pierce. My father said I would be christened in the Episcopal church. He was an ardent non-church-attending Episcopalian, of which the world still has a few. I was christened according to his wishes. But compliance did not come easily to my mother for she was a stanch indoctrinated unequivocal vociferous Baptist. All of her family were Baptist. My grandfather Brown had two distinctions: he had been a captain in the Confederate Army and he was a Baptist. My grandmother Brown had three distinctions: her father had been a Baptist minister, she had married a captain in the Confederate Army, and she was a Baptist. My mother acquiesced to the christening because she felt that so small an amount of water and the kindly ministrations of Archdeacon Cresson could do me no harm, while surely when I reached the age of spiritual accountability, which the Baptists arbitrarily set at twelve, I would forego confirmation for true salvation and immersion. Which I did. But in the interim delightful old Mr. Cresson, who roved up and down the Indian River in a sailboat keeping the scattered Episcopalians in line, was one of my heroes.

I remember my father largely because of his love for books. He introduced me to Dickens, Scott, Thackeray and was no doubt responsible for my own addiction to books. Also I recall him as a stimulating person, independent in thought for his day. He shared with my uncle Arthur Brown, editor of *the* newspaper in Fort Pierce, an intense interest in the coming of the railroads to Florida. In my grade school days I recall the reflected excitement of the drainage of the Everglades, freed of malaria and yellow fever, making possible the extension of the railway to Key West. The first train reached Miami in '96.

If I had psychic experience in my childhood I was unaware of the fact. Anything unorthodox would have been frowned out of me while a religious vision or an angelic prophecy would have been bragged into my consciousness, but looking back I realize that I was often aware what people were going to say before they spoke and aware what they were thinking when they did not speak. Also I recognized untruthfulness so that I sometimes wondered why people bothered to lie when it was so apparent they were not being honest, and yet other people were often deceived. In our community, the nearest demonstrable approach to the psychic was the phenomenon of conversion which occupied the center of community interest.

Our entire social life centered in the church. Sundays

were given over to Sunday School and Church in the morning, followed by an ample dinner, a drowsy interlude, and then a kind of children's mission circle called the Sunbeam Band, a respite, a supper in the kitchen—my favorite meal of the week because one helped himself to all of the tasty leftovers of Sunday dinner—and then the evening service. The evening service was an institution in itself. It was there the minister put on the rousements. At night the congregational singing was twice as lusty—

When the trumpet of the Lord shall sound
And time shall be no more,
When the morning breaks eternal bright and fair,
When the saved of earth shall gather
Over on the other shore,
And the roll is called up yonder
I'll be there.

I hoped I would be there! Although we sang of heaven the preacher preached on hell, and I never heard of anyone's being saved through longing to reach heaven.

Some neighbor children contributed more to my theology than all the preachers of my boyhood. Across the river from my home there was a Coast Guard Station known as the House of Refuge, manned by a French Canadian who had several sons who were my schoolmates and with whom I played on Saturdays—those wonderful year-long Saturdays which bridged the routine of school and the responsibility of Sunday. One boy, a stocky agile chap about my own age, later became one of my closest associates although I never saw him after we were about nine years old. Under an assumed name he is now known to everyone who ever had a professional sitting with me.

His family were Roman Catholics, the only Catholics

so far as I knew in our general neighborhood. My mother
did not like to have me play with them. After all, what did
the Baptist church save one from if not hell and Romanism?
But I was fascinated by the way these French Canadian
boys referred to the saints as if they were living personalities, and highly useful at that. My own ideas of life after
death were shaped by the kind of preaching to which I
was exposed, exposition based on the Biblical steps of salvation—faith, repentance, baptism—which prepared one
for a safe death after which one was judged on one's record
and admitted to heaven or sent to eternal damnation. But
these Roman Catholic boys talked about an intermediate
state called purgatory from which the dead, if not too
wicked, might be rescued by the prayers of their friends
augmented by the payment of money to the priest. Even
though I was informed by my mother that some pope had
invented the whole idea of purgatory as a way to extract
money from the gullible, still it appealed to me and I hoped
that if I died in that in-between state of goodness and bad-
ness where I felt myself usually to be, I would perhaps have
friends who would say those prayers. As for the saints,
it seemed reasonable that if they had once served mankind,
they might continue to care for the needy. And why not the
other living dead who had been members of my own family?
There was my great-grandfather Pigue in South Carolina,
for instance, who was known for his kindness to his slaves
—would he not put in a word for a great-grandson who
expected to be a minister?

My mother and most of my friends seemed to take it for
granted that I would enter the ministry, as the phrase had
it, so my expectation followed theirs. By the time I was
twelve I played the piano for the meetings of the Baptist
Young People's Union, known as the BYPU, attended all
services, and one bright Sunday joined the church. For me

there was no emotional experience about it; at the expected time I merely did the expected thing.

But perhaps I had been prompted somewhat by an evangelist who had preached on "The Unpardonable Sin." He did not define the unpardonable sin but he sent me home feeling I had committed it. If in the night an unusual noise wakened me I waited for the devil to appear.

Up to the time of my conversion no one I cared about had died, and then one day a certain woman, who did not attend church and to whom my mother and her friends referred as "that woman," committed suicide. She was one of the prettiest women in our section of the country and there was always about her the scent of perfume even when she was not going to a party. We children thought she was wonderful because whenever we ran into her at the drugstore she bought us ice cream sodas. I never understood why all the women of the community were down on her. My mother, in spite of her dislike for the woman, was one of those who volunteered to "lay her out." It puzzled me that my mother should go to so much trouble to bathe and dress a dead woman to whom she would not speak in life.

Then I remembered my Catholic friends' talk of purgatory and I sensed that surely there must be some further chance for the woman's salvation. I decided to pray for her. I remember feeling comforted, altogether more at ease in my world, because I could still help her. It was years later that I discovered the passages in the Bible which enjoin us to pray for the dead.

The annual revival not only introduced me to the subject of death but also to the problem of sex. It was a custom for the evangelist to have one meeting for men and boys only. Now I found out for the first time why the women of the town did not like my popular friend for whom I prayed; she had never settled on one husband. When I got home my father, who took a superior attitude toward revival meetings, asked me what the evangelist had said. I repeated the preacher's generalities, after which my father, not at all embarrassed, told me the facts of life. He had a sane view of sex and for the first time the subject appeared as a normal interest and not the evil ugly thing I had deduced. My father gave me Hawthorne's *The Scarlet Letter*. It was rather heavy reading but it planted in my consciousness a tolerance of human weakness for which I have always been grateful. And obliquely it gave me reassurance that my prayers for the woman who committed suicide would be answered.

About this time the Northerners were beginning to discover Florida as a winter resort. We called them damnyankees, all one word. All the damnyankees seemed to have money. These were prosperous days toward the end of the second Theodore Roosevelt presidency. We had a large house and my mother rented rooms to the enterprising tourists.

I was about fifteen when I found in a room vacated by an especially charming old couple two booklets which had a lot to do with shaping my future. One of them was *The Metropolitan Opera News* and the other a little pamphlet called *Evolution and Religion* by J. T. Sunderland, published by the King's Chapel, a Unitarian church in Boston. Both of these booklets revealed new worlds to me and both stated that future publications could be had, free, by sending in one's name. Immediately I was on their mailing lists. Thereafter I received the weekly sermon from King's Chapel and a monthly report of what was going on in the world of music. My father and I read the sermons together while my mother confiscated them when she could. What I understood of the Unitarian point of view, I liked. Moreover, I spread my new views around. In fact, I became such a heretic that I refused to play the piano for the BYPU. Although I read and discussed this offbeat literature, still it never occurred to me that I was not a good Baptist. Being a Baptist was like being a Democrat; everyone who was anyone *was*. He might strain at the leash and argue for reform but the fold was his birthright. And then one day I was called before a meeting of the deacons and elders of my church for interrogation as to my beliefs. I found out that the Word of God as printed in good plain English was to be accepted as understood by one's fellow church members and no questions asked about the way in which members of other communions read that same Word. Although I was not very skillful in answering their arguments, I knew that something tremendous was eluding my interrogators and I knew I could not abide within their boundaries. When I left that meeting I was "churched" which was Southern Baptist for excommunicated. At sixteen.

My mother was more embarrassed than crushed. My father took no part in the controversy. He had long since got beyond sectarianism; I felt that he was not disapproving.

About this time a number of families from the North moved to town, among them a retired clergyman by the name of Simpson. These people did not join any of the local churches but simply called themselves Christians and started to hold services in the Odd Fellows Hall. They talked about church unity, and expressed the conviction that anyone who felt himself to be a follower of Jesus had a right to take part in Holy Communion which they called the Lord's Supper. This was scandalous doctrine to the close-communion Baptists. I talked with Mr. Simpson about my interest in the Unitarian sermons. He knew about Unitarians and felt they had something to contribute to Christian unity. None of the sects unduly perturbed him. He was a man who could stake his own claim without putting up fences. When I was seventeen I decided to join the Christian church. And this move, surprisingly, determined my ensuing education.

Our local high school had only a two-year course, but Mr. Simpson told me of an academy in Tennessee where I could work my way and finish high school. So I took the savings I had earned from the usual Saturday and summer odd jobs, bought a ticket, and departed for Johnson Academy, Kimberlin Heights, Tennessee, with forty dollars in my pocket.

Johnson Academy was run by faith. The teachers received their salaries according as the Lord prospered the institution. We ate on the same terms. Principal and teachers were ardent in prayer, besides which the principal made trips among the churches to let the loyal know that we were living by prayer. Each of us boys had a list of donors for whom we prayed. I became known as one of the most effective pray-ers in the school. However, my success in prayer was not unrelated to the job by which I earned my keep. Most of the boys worked on the large Academy farm, but since I could type and was good at figures I worked in the office and one of my tasks was making up the lists of names to be prayed for. I am afraid I placed on my own list some of the likeliest prospects. Nevertheless I did pray earnestly and some of my more unlikely prospects came through with gifts.

One of my prayers was for a chance to go to college. In the fall of 1917 I entered Transylvania on a scholarship. I also went into the Reserve Officers Training Corps. Being a ministerial student I was exempt from the draft but along with most of the rest of college-America I felt it my patriotic duty to rescue Belgian babies from German atrocities. But I never got overseas. My psychic experience was the nearest I came to catastrophe—but it had left me battle-scarred.

CHAPTER 3

Exploring the Psychic

LIKE A GOOD MANY other persons who find they have some
psychic projection, I was very willing to experiment but
did not know how to begin. Neither did Professor Snoddy.
We tried table-tipping and got some apparently responsible personalities from what was commonly called "the
other side." Sometimes I was able to come up with clairvoyant knowledge but of no great moment. Blindfolded
I was sometimes able to tell what he was doing across the
room and at times to tell what he was thinking. It did not
occur to us to try hypnotism, although Snoddy had read
some of the excellent European literature on the subject.

We took some care who was in on our experiments.
Professor Snoddy early warned me not to broadcast my
Camp Grant experience in the college community; it was
enough to have come out for higher criticism and evolution. During the winter he loaned me books on psychic
matters and on mysticism. In a way the latter books interested me the more. I was astounded to find that many of the
world's religious geniuses had had psychic powers, among
them Wesley, Luther, Swedenborg, Dwight Moody, not
to overlook a high proportion of the saints. Snoddy had a
theory that lives devoted to finding God developed this out-

reach; he had fine-combed Wesley's *Journals* and *Letters* and noted the way in which Wesley expected God to manifest himself in special power and often found his expectations realized. On the other hand, I would point out, not many missionaries seemed to have psychic insight or healing power, and Snoddy would scratch his head and wonder if it was not possible to be serving God so diligently with one's eyes on the task at hand that one forgot to look to the Source as avidly as had some of the saints. He felt strongly that a life of prayer led to an extension of awareness which often reached the proportions of clairvoyance and clairaudience.

But then there was the fact that unholy persons also had psychic gifts. This was a poser, but Snoddy's reading took him into Eastern religions where the documentation on the methods of extending psychic abilities was abundant. Evidently the laws of development could work at many levels. Fortunately we had the sense to know that we needed guidance, both human and divine.

After a time we invited Dr. Alonzo W. Fortune, pastor of Lexington's largest Christian Church, to join us. Dr. Fortune was not only the greatest preacher I had heard up to that time, but also a sound scholar in the New Testament field, as well as one of the most understanding and lovable of men. He had recently published a book, *The Conception of Authority in the Pauline Writings*, and he pointed out to me that Paul had no acquaintance with the historical Jesus but that his knowledge of Jesus and his loyalty to Him stemmed from his own arresting psychic experience, beginning with his vision on the road to Damascus. Gradually Dr. Fortune and St. Paul between them gave me a feeling of being "called" to develop whatever unusual gifts might come my way. I remember that Dr. Fortune read me the twelfth and thirteenth chapters of First Corinthians, insisting that they should always be read together, and emphasizing Paul's approval of the spiritual "gifts," such as precognition and nonmedical healing, so long as love dominated their use. I felt an undefined but deep-seated dedication rise in me which I wish I had always maintained.

I read up on the proceedings of the Society for Psychical Research in Britain, which had come into being scarcely a decade before my birth. It impressed me that the Society had been founded by distinguished men of science and letters who were fundamentally interested in finding an answer to the philosophical question: Is the universe friendly? The answer, they felt, was bound in some degree to findings on the continuity of personality beyond death: if achievement in life could hope to be extended in a longer time span, then the universe had meaning. Frederick W. H. Myers, a classical scholar of wide reputation who had been the first to bring Freud to the attention of British scholars, was particularly interested in the problem of what constitutes consciousness. Professor Snoddy had Myers' six-hundred-page documentation *Human Personality and Its Survival of Bodily Death* and this I read with avidity.

Both Snoddy and Fortune knew something about the work of the American Society for Psychical Research but both were scholars in other fields and had little time, really, to give to these matters. We read some of the literature on the Piper case, as the long and careful investigation of this Boston medium was called. Her mediumship had come upon her when she visited a study group interested in the development of clairvoyance; falling into a brief trance she had written a message for Judge Frost of Cambridge, a noted jurist, which he felt could have come from no one but his dead son. Not long afterward, William James' mother-in-law had gone to see her and had reported such supernormal abilities on the part of the medium that finally Professor James himself had gone to investigate, and there began a series of investigations which engaged the attention of some of the foremost minds in England and America. I was impressed again by the quality of the men who were interested, even more than by their thoroughness. One might expect such men to be meticulous for they carried over the disciplines of their own various fields, but that they should consider supernormal powers of the mind not only genuine but important struck deep into my thinking.

Two or three of my fraternity brothers became interested in psychic matters; one of them knew a man in his home town who could diagnose while in trance; doctors had tested the man and had proved that he could get at the cause of disease clairvoyantly. Another knew an old woman who could tell what the weather would be a year in advance; she was sometimes consulted before dates were set for the county fair. We began to accumulate a few reports we felt to be reliable. Also when we heard of a good fortuneteller, we went. A gypsy picked me out of a crowd and told me I had "the gift."

One of those boys, a chap named Joe, took his psychic interests seriously. When he became very ill with pneumonia and the doctors gave up hope for his recovery, he called me over and in his last labored breaths said to me, "If I can get back I'll give you proof." I must say I never expected to hear from Joe again. But some months later when I was on vacation in Michigan I attended a Spiritualist meeting at which the clairvoyant pointed to me and told me that a friend on the other side had a message for me. She described Joe in detail, although she could not get his name, and said he was talking about dynamite. Such a message made no sense to me and I wrote off the clairvoyant for dealing in trivia. But a year later another psychic repeated the performance. Still a year later a third psychic in another state described Joe and insisted he was saying a word that sounded like dynamite, although not exactly dynamite. She said my friend wanted me to say the word with him, he saying the first syllable, I the second and he the third.

Then I knew what he wanted. The word was *Dynamus*, the secret password of the fraternity to which we both belonged, and as a means of identification the word was lettered back and forth between the brothers, along with the grip. The password changed each year, but the year Joe had died it had been *Dynamus*. My friend was proving himself in the way he had been accustomed to do in life. But this incident still lay ahead of me; while in college I had my moments of skepticism about survival.

In the summer of 1921 I made a trip to New York to see the work of the American Society for Psychical Research. One of the first persons I met was Miss Gertrude Tubby, then secretary of the organization. She not only knew the men currently prominent but she made the history of the Society's work come alive for me, for she had been in touch with it since the days of William James and Stanley Hall. During the years when Professor James H. Hyslop directed the program Miss Tubby had been his man Friday, his trusted envoy on research jaunts, his representative and amanuensis at hundreds of rigidly controlled seances, and most of all his steadfast friend.

She also knew Dr. Franklin Prince very well, of course. He had assumed charge of the ASPR program after Hyslop's death. She arranged for me to meet him. He was already widely known for his careful work on the multiple personality case of Doris Fischer, but the faculty that impressed me was not his thoroughness so much as his skepticism. Nothing remained proven for Prince if he could find an opening for one more question mark.

That trip to New York provided a foundation for my

future study. I became a member of the American Society and from then on got all of its publications. Miss Tubby also sent me many books she felt would be of interest.

Just the same my greatest excitement lay in preaching and I began to preach as a student minister in churches near Lexington. I liked preaching. Looking back, I realize how earnest I was, and how young. I also had a new extracurricular interest: I fell in love. Kentucky was noted for its beautiful girls. The next year I married one of the nicest.

In my junior year I was called to St. Matthew's Church, near Louisville, to substitute for a year during the minister's absence, and not long after our arrival one of the deacons very timidly asked me if I knew anything about spiritualism. Cautiously I acknowledged that I did. A shade bolder, he asked a few questions. A mite more audacious, I told a few of my experiences. He then astonished me by saying that a small group in the church was sitting once a week, experimenting at table-tipping. Would I join them? I would. Our meetings were secret. It was during these sessions that I was first hypnotized. On several occasions I did approximate trance but none of us knew what to do with the trance state once it was achieved.

Fortunately reports of my preaching got around faster and further than news of my psychic interests. I was called to a county seat church at Barbourville in southern Kentucky. For a young minister it was an excellent opening, but it was also a full-time job and if I accepted I would have to drop out of college in my senior year. Feeling like something of a heretic because I had changed my views from some of the more orthodox thinking of my denomination, I talked the matter over with Dr. Fortune. He thought I ought to take the church. Furthermore, he felt I should be ordained, even though I had not been graduated. His advice prevailed and in 1922, along with a number of other young ministers, I was ordained by Alonzo Fortune and I. J. Spencer in the Chestnut Street Christian Church of Lexington. It was a moving experience.

During our second year in Barbourville, Dr. Paul Pearson, founder and president of the Swarthmore Chautauqua Association of Pennsylvania, came to town. He was a distinguished Quaker and he ran his three big circuits through New England, the Eastern states and part of the South as a great educational venture. He was on his way to visit "Burns of the Mountains," a genial and compassionate man afraid of nothing, who had started a school in the mountains in an attempt to shed the light of reason on the bloody feuds which had raged for generations. Pearson wanted Burns to come out and tell his story to the Chautauqua audiences.

Since Dr. Pearson was in town on Sunday he came to hear me preach. We invited him to dinner and he then invited me to go with him some forty miles on horseback to find Burns. During our trip I found out that Pearson was interested in psychic matters. He told me about his friend, Sir Oliver Lodge, who had recently lectured in America in response to the widespread interest in his book *Raymond,* the story of his communication with his son who had been killed in the World War. He also talked about Sir Arthur Conan Doyle who had been lecturing widely in this country. In view of the interest they had created, Dr. Pearson felt it would be worthwhile to present a popular lecture on psychical matters on his New England circuit. Before he left town he had signed me on to do this job.

I was glad that I could leave Barbourville on a wave of appreciation. In the two years of my ministry the membership had more than doubled, a fine pipe organ had been installed, a director of music added to the staff, and an educational department completed. The church was harmonious throughout. I would not have thought, at that time, of adding the fact that many members of my congregation were taking seriously the implications of personal immortality for moral responsibility on this earth. I was asked to name my successor, which I did. I am sure I shall always feel myself to be a part of that church.

My marriage had not been successful. Looking back, I can see that neither of us was ready for marriage. I was definitely more interested in intellectual concerns than in my home. My wife felt that I neglected her for the church and I did. When it came to going East, even in summer, she preferred to stay with her parents; they were always the center of her life; psychologically she had never left home. We parted for the summer without plans for permanent separation but without sorrow. We never got together again and some time later we were divorced.

I was off to New England and my first lecture tour.

CHAPTER 4

The Training of a Psychic

ALL THAT SUMMER of 1924 I toured New England and the Eastern states, speaking to large audiences of interested and friendly people. The title of my lecture was "The Witching Hour." I know now it must have been a superficial sort of presentation of the field of psychical research but it was sound, as well as dramatic. I was surprised to find that after almost every lecture someone, and sometimes several, came up to tell me about firsthand experiences they knew of or had had.

At the end of the season Dr. Pearson asked me to stay on for his winter lecture service. My headquarters would be in New York. I accepted. I still expected to go back into the ministry, but for the time being I intended to learn as much as I could in the psychic field.

Fortunately I had Miss Tubby to turn to.

It is highly important, but also unusual, for a young and eager psychic to have such introductions and practical training as Miss Tubby could provide. I was in the hands of a hardheaded, indefatigable expert. She saw to it that I not only met the researchers but got to sit with mediums of repute.

Having a living to earn, I continued on the lecture

platform and my lectures about psychic matters took on a bit of authenticity because I could speak from increasingly broad experience of my own. It was about this time that I ran upon an unexpected chapter of my own family history. One night I dropped into a meeting where a psychic was doing some open reading. He described my father and grandfather, then both dead, and reported that they were insistently saying a word that sounded like *neversink.* *Neversink.* He ran the words together, emphatically. Certainly the message meant nothing to me and I wrote off the medium.

A few weeks after the *neversink* message I was in a small town in the western part of New York State when I saw a road sign: TEN MILES TO NEVERSINK. There was that word again. The short of it is that I went to the village of Neversink and after inquiry was directed to a very old lady named Lucy Ford Hornbeck. She readily described her brother, Albert Ford, who had died some years previous, and showed me his photograph. There was my grandfather with my grandmother and my father, then a boy; the same photograph my father had treasured all his life. It seems my grandfather had not been drowned when his ship was wrecked but had been injured and ill. By the time he got back to Florida he could find no trace of his wife and son. Those were the tumultuous reconstruction days. Concluding that they were dead, he returned and lived to a ripe old age in New York State. It was from this great-aunt that I found out that my great-grandfather had anglicized the name Fordeaux upon becoming an American citizen. So my mother, of Huguenot descent, had married a Frenchman. Some way I had always supposed the name Ford to be Irish.

Next to Miss Tubby the most helpful friend I had in New York City those first years was Robert Norwood, then rector of St. Bartholomew's Episcopal Church. I had first met him in Swarthmore, the headquarters for Dr. Pearson's Chautauqua. He had a church near there and he and Pearson were great friends. In fact, he had lectured for a season on the Chautauqua circuit. He used to invite me along with others to join him on Sunday evenings after evensong. The first time I went to supper I noticed that there was a place at the table which was unoccupied, and later I learned that this place was always set for a son of the Norwoods who had died tragically in their Canadian summer camp. The family simply refused to look on death as separation and always considered the son a part of the family circle. Later in New York it was Norwood who introduced me to some of his friends who were interested in psychic matters. Some of them are still among my closest friends.

Not only was Dr. Norwood a great preacher; he was a mystic in the true sense. He used to tell me that during his church service, he was often aware of unseen persons, both swelling his congregation and standing beside him in the pulpit. He said he had come so to depend upon the participation of unseen ministers that he would frequently prepare only the outline of his sermon, then ask that someone of a higher dimension join forces with him and often he would feel himself spoken through, swept by ideas he had never before thought and using illustrations which had never before come into his mind. He knew that people felt the power emanating from his pulpit and he knew the power did not come from him. I always felt humble in Norwood's company, and also stimulated; often inspired.

Before I had been long in New York I got acquainted with some of the Spiritualist groups. By that time I had found out that, according to the definition adopted by the

National Spiritualist Association of America, spiritualism is "the science, philosophy and religion of continuous life, based upon the demonstrated fact of communication, by means of mediumship, with those who live in the Spirit World." Young and fresh from a pastorate in a denomination known for its empirical approach to religion, it then seemed to me a very sad thing that people should have to found a special church to feel at ease in speaking frankly and confidently of the basic concept of immortality.

As I watched other mediums I naturally caught on to something of their methods. I found that when awake I could bring myself into a half-hypnotized state in which I could stand before an audience and describe unseen presences and often pick up their messages. Spiritualist groups began to ask me to speak for them and to do this open clairvoyance. I knew that I needed more training but in lieu of training I practiced on the audiences.

About this time I met a man named Francis R. Fast, who became one of the great friends of my life. He was a businessman who acted for many of the Hawaiian sugar interests. Although he was considerably older than I, and his family grown, we became close associates in our program of psychic investigation. He was a man of character in the old-fashioned meaning of the word. As time went on he took over my financial affairs.

Francis Fast was an active member of the ASPR and through him I met several persons who were trying to develop their psychic faculties. This was a new idea to me, that there were exercises which could be done consistently for the specific purpose of increasing awareness. We formed a class in spiritual unfoldment, not too accurate a term, for it was our psychic abilities which were being unfolded rather than our spiritual powers. It was here with this group that I learned to relax the body, a much rarer art than the average person supposes. I also learned the beginning of a method of concentration.

Work in this class prepared me for the next necessary step. I found a teacher. The East has it that when a student is ready the teacher appears, and this is undoubtedly a general fact of spiritual life. I needed help and it came in the form of an introduction to Paramhansa Yogananda, a distinguished Indian philosopher.

Swami Yogananda had come to America in the fall of 1920 to address a meeting of religious liberals under the auspices of the American Unitarian Association in Boston. When I met him I realized that here was a man who had the answers to many of my needs. I told Swami Yogananda that I needed help in learning how to meditate, how to become unattached so that I could be aware of truth, how to use a trance. It did not occur to me to try to find some teacher in the Protestant tradition who could give me such help. Swami Yogananda accepted me, not so much as student in any formal sense of the word, but as friend. Such powers as mine were nothing new to him, nor did he rate them as significant except as they might be used to deepen awareness.

I often traveled a considerable distance to hear him lecture, for he never failed to challenge the commonplace. From him I learned that truth belongs to neither East nor West, but is a universal thing, which only seems different when one does not look beneath its varying cultural expressions. Yogananda was constantly trying to show the interrelatedness of mankind's problems; he never imposed Eastern attitudes or methods. For instance, when I asked him if I should learn the Eastern *asanas*, or attitudes of prayer, he replied, "Yoga means simply union with God, a state for which all men strive, but it is not necessary to adopt the classical yoga methods to succeed in finding God.

The Christian tradition of kneeling in prayer is an *asana:* use the postures to which you are accustomed. Never let methods become an end, they are only important as they help you attain results."

Some of his followers were forever wanting definitive statements of his teaching, but he would smile his warm encompassing smile and insist, "Men are bound together and to God by eternal principles which they have to discover; words which try to define these principles more often than not confuse and divide."

Once I remember going to Yogananda with some question about free will and determinism or fate. He treated all questions seriously, in the spirit in which they were asked, and never made a beginner feel like a fool. He said in effect, "Fate, karma, destiny—call it what you will—there is a law of justice which somehow, but not by chance, determines our race, our physical structure and some of our mental and emotional traits. These are mediated to us through our genes, but the important thing to realize is that while we may not escape our own basic pattern, we can work in conformity with it. That is where free will comes in. We are free to choose and discriminate to the limits of our understanding, and as we rightly exercise our power of choice, our understanding grows. Then once having chosen, a man has to accept the consequences of his choice and go on from there."

In the ensuing years Yogananda attracted a large following in America. At Encinitas, California, a beautiful temple was built for his discourses, with caves for meditation and a hotel for the convenience of those who studied with him. In the early twenties in New York, when he was teaching me to slip into a self-induced trance in place of having to be hypnotized, I did not understand the dimension of the man nor of his teaching. No doubt he knew that and left me to my fate and free will!

I accepted an invitation to lecture for a time in the First Spiritualist Church of New York City which met on Sunday evenings in Carnegie Hall. I was fortunate in that this was a critical audience, accustomed to hearing more distinguished men than I and to seeing excellent demonstrations of psychic gifts. So I had to extend myself and work at my own development. At that time, before I had finished my studies with Swami Yogananda, my mediumship was still somewhat sporadic and I never knew whether I would get results or not. When strangers wanted to reach their departed relatives through me, I was willing to be the go-between, but sometimes no relatives appeared! How was I to know whether the relatives refused to communicate with their earth-bound family or whether I was not properly geared for transmission? In other words, was the line down, or was there just no one at its other end? Usually, however, in a public meeting some of those persons in the audience had relatives ready to converse.

I found that my main task on such occasions was to make myself open to whatever might come through. Soon the result was a fairly consistent ability to stand before an audience, half block out the people before me, feel as if I were about to go into trance but not lose consciousness, and then let discarnate personalities either appear before me or impress me with a description of themselves while at the same time I heard, wordlessly, the messages they wished to convey.

Whenever I threw my critical mind into a skeptical mood, telling myself, "This man couldn't be named Gregory Klegory Tegory," and tried to substitute something which sounded more sensible, then I misfired. But when I went ahead and reported what I heard or saw, the result was usually a response from someone in the audience.

Although I was doing a fair amount of public work, I thought of myself as an amateur and fully intended to go into some other profession as soon as I learned a little more about the reach of the mind. I remember the day I realized that my own psychic powers no longer seemed strange. If I had been looking for an analogy I suppose I would have said that now I felt like a horse with its blinders off. I was less hedged in. The universe had widened. Most of all, life made more sense, for apparently death did not put an end to man's strivings nor to his concern for his loved ones.

As my public work increased I used to wish there were some way to hold back the crowds of discarnates who pressed about me. Sometimes I "saw" them, sometimes I felt them, but either way there were often too many of them. There should be some method, or someone, to keep them in order, to determine precedence. I had to take whomever clamored the loudest, silent though the clamor might be. What was needed was an invisible master of ceremonies. It was at this point that a partner came into my life and Fletcher became my right-hand man.

CHAPTER 5

Fletcher

ONE DAY IN 1924 when I was in trance an invisible personality announced himself as Fletcher and said that henceforth he would be my permanent assistant on the unseen plane. Just that simply our partnership began. Fletcher said he was able to work efficiently with me because he had the right energy pitch or frequency for establishing and maintaining contact. It was years before I had anything like a consistent notion of what he was talking about, but I was delighted that I was to have a dependable colleague who would appear whenever I went into trance and act as interlocutor between the invisible and visible visitors who came to talk together through my intermediacy. Such a partner is commonly called a "control." Of course it was not I to whom Fletcher spoke directly; he announced himself to a friend of mine who was having the sitting—"Tell Ford that I am to be his control and that I go by the name of Fletcher." At the next sitting my friend asked him, for me, who he was and for what personal reason he had attached himself to me in this helpful manner. Fletcher then explained that he was one of the French Canadian boys who had lived across the river from my home in Fort Pierce. He wished to use his middle name, Fletcher, he said, in order to save his family possible embarrassment because they were Roman Catholics and had certain ideas of the hereafter which did not exactly fit with what he had found. They might even be disturbed, he said, to know that he had not found heaven to be inhabited exclusively by persons of his own faith; indeed, he himself had at first been very much surprised. He said further that after the family left Fort Pierce he had grown up in Canada, had enlisted in the World War and had been killed in action. He named his company and the place of his death; also he gave the address of his family.

I wrote to the family, asking after various members, including this boy, but not mentioning of course that I had heard from him directly. One of the boys answered telling me of his brother's death, corroborating Fletcher's statement as to time and place. So I accepted Fletcher at his (invisible) face value. At times, however, I do see him and always as a young man. Sometimes when I am giving a public demonstration and am not actually in trance, his face appears vividly before me.

We soon had a fine working partnership. When I wish to go into trance I lie down on a couch or lean back in a comfortable chair and breathe slowly and rhythmically until I feel an in-drawing of energy at the solar plexus. Then I focus my attention on Fletcher's face as I have come to know it, until gradually I feel as if his face presses into my own at which instant there is a sense of shock somewhat as if I were passing out. Then I lose consciousness, appearing to be asleep. My body is in a state of sleep and when I waken at the end of a session I feel as if I had had a good nap.

As soon as I am in trance, Fletcher announces his arrival to the sitters in the room by saying "hello" in a slightly French Canadian accent. Obviously it is my speaking equipment he is using, and for the most part my vocabulary. Sometimes he uses words given him by discarnates but the fact that he catches an impressive word does not mean he can pronounce it correctly. Sometimes he spells out a specialized word as it is apparently being spelled to him; at other times he attempts two or three pronunciations until he seems to get an inner nod of approval that he has said the word correctly.

During the first moments of the trance Fletcher appears to size up the sitters. He may comment upon their geographic derivation. "You come from my part of the country." "I see you've just flown in from the west coast." "You seem to be quite a traveler." Or he may say, "You're a chemist." "You spend a lot of time at an easel." "Another preacher tonight." Or perhaps, "The worried man in the corner." "The woman with a pencil." He has even been known to correct the spelling of a sitter on the opposite side of the room from the sleeping medium. He may ask the first names of the sitters and perhaps add, "The middle initial is X; that's an odd one."

The names of the invisibles are sometimes difficult for Fletcher to get, as for any control. He may feel around trying Harry, Henry, finally coming out with, "No, he shakes his head; ah, it is Harrall." On one occasion when a discarnate medical man was asked by a sitter to pick out the individual in the room who needed medical aid, the invisible physician immediately indicated the patient but had to feel around for her first name. "Her name is—let me see —it is summer, the fields are lush and green, everything is in full bloom—oh, yes, her name is June." On another occasion when Fletcher was trying to get across the identity of a woman on the unseen side but could not seem to catch her name, he remarked, "They're showing me a book . . . it's a book of poetry . . . by Longfellow. It's about my part of the country. Acadia! Oh, the name is Evangeline."

Sometimes amusing dislocations happen. For instance, a

rather saintly minister, discarnate, was reported by Fletcher as saying that a current family situation was a blankety-blank shame. After the sitting the horrified daughter protested that her father had never in his life used profanity. When he was really angry, she said, he sometimes used the word *tarnation* and then they all got out of his way. This kind of dislocation is apparently a part of the problem of translating emotional impact into words.

Who in the unseen world comes to the seances? First of all, the loved ones of the sitter. Most persons who come to a medium have someone they care for who has died, with whom they wish to make contact. If that individual is interested and available he is probably waiting at the threshold and may be the first person Fletcher describes and introduces. Usually the invisible relative or friend wants first to identify himself, and often does so by calling the sitter by a nickname or referring to other members of the family by traits known only to the family; or he mentions key incidents in the past, incidents often known only to the sitter and the one communicating. The wealth of evidence brought through may be considerable. And among the best of the evidential is often some trivia which the sitter has forgotten and brushes aside as inaccurate. I have found that it never pays to refuse any data; just make notes and wait. Later the items under suspicion may prove the most valuable evidence of continuing consciousness.

For instance, one night in the winter of 1955 I attended a dinner party in Rye, New York. There were a dozen guests, among them the guest of honor, Dr. William T. Bidwell, of Greenville, South Carolina. After dinner we sat in the library. I was seated alone on one of the davenports and being full of good food, I was drowsy and fell into a clairvoyant but not unconscious state. I recall that a guest from New Jersey discovered that he and a guest from Connecticut had a common friend and someone made the usual remark about the smallness of the world.

Then I spoke up, "There is a man here who gives his name as Adams and he says how right you are. He says his old home is only a couple of blocks from Dr. Bidwell's home in Greenville and that he knew the Browns in China." (I am borrowing the name Brown.) Dr. Bidwell said he never heard of this man Adams; Mr. and Mrs. Brown said they never heard of him either. Someone chided me, remarking that even a medium couldn't always be right. But a few minutes later Mr. Brown walked over to the bookcase and took down an issue of *Who's Who*. There was the name Walter Alexander Adams; the permanent address was Greenville, about two blocks from Dr. Bidwell's home; the man Adams had been first vice-consul both in Nanking and Tsingtao when the Browns lived there in the early twenties. They could not have helped but know him in that small foreign community.

Most discarnates intent upon reaching their loved ones still living on earth want more than anything to establish the fact that they are not dead; next they usually want to send their love, to manifest the emotional bond which keeps them in contact with those they care for. Hence most messages are personal, concrete, more or less trivial. That is, the average invisible does not make philosophical pronouncements or divulge epochal scientific knowledge, and for the best of reasons; he would not speak in those terms if he were meeting his family face to face. He evidences much the same interests he had on earth, with one exception.

The exception which creeps into a high percentage of the messages is the fact that the invisibles want their earth friends to know that their plane of consciousness, their situation as "dead" persons, is nothing like the stereotype of heaven. Only a few bother to be coherent about what their state *is* like, but then very few sitters ask consistent questions. The only people vaguer than the dead are the living. It never ceases to amaze me that so few ministers, who spend their lives comforting the dying and consoling the bereaved, who speak eloquently about Easter and promise salvation in terms of eternal life, should have so little intelligent curiosity about the nature of death and the afterlife. Most of them do not even have a tentative hypothesis. Nor does the average person who comes for a sitting.

Apparently discarnate friends, sensing the general ignorance and lack of interest, do not try to enlighten the incurious in the short hour or so afforded by mediumistic communication. And how could they when the whole subject of the nature of consciousness is involved? However, a discarnate will sometimes do his best to inform a sitter that the communication between them could be direct. Sometimes the message is heeded and the living person will put some effort into developing his own pick-up in the form of clairaudience, automatic writing or trance. After all, there are thousands who know this direct communication one way and another.

Besides family and friends, specialists of various kinds show up in response to specific requests for specific aid. But the specialists appear to be acquaintances of the interrogator or of some discarnate friend of the interrogator's friend! They do not just appear uninvited because a sitter needs legal aid, say, or psychological counseling. Invisible promotors of causes sometimes arrive to give counsel to earth friends who are interested in the same cause; editors pop in on the seance of a writer, but usually because of some former contact, direct or by way of a mutual acquaintance, living or discarnate.

Fletcher does not seem to move aimlessly back and forth between the visible and invisible worlds. In terms of place, he does not seem to move at all, and is always insisting that the universe is one and that the invisibles are not in another place but only in another state of consciousness. Or, as a discarnate husband recently remarked to a grieving wife when she was bewailing having been left alone, "I haven't gone anywhere."

Now it is one thing to state that Fletcher exists as a personality separate from my own personality and to describe his ostensible method of acting as a go-between, and it is something quite different to explain how he operates. This is a question I am often asked—the process which enables a discarnate personality to impress a "living" mind.

The customary explanation is that the mind of the entranced medium becomes passive and the mind of the discarnate who acts as control then takes possession of the body mechanism of the medium; using the medium's speaking apparatus but his own mental equipment, the control reports what he "sees" and "hears" among other discarnates and is also able to comment upon things going on in the room. Thus, in trance I would be said to be mentally quiescent, blacked out, while Fletcher in some way takes over the physical mechanism which controls my hearing and speaking. This explanation sounds reasonable enough, in broad terms, if one does not press for particulars.

However, I have a sitter who is a persistent questioner. For months she pressed questions about aspects of consciousness, to which she got only a general response. But her persistence must have attracted the attention of some discarnate intelligences who wished to co-operate in giving her more of an answer. One day a discarnate personality who gave her name as Ruth Finley spoke out at a group sitting and said she was interested in working with this inquiring woman. Mrs. Finley identified herself further as the Joan of the Darby and Joan disclosures, the publication of which had led to her work with Betty and Stewart White before Mrs. White's death, and afterward with Mr. White and his discarnate wife in receiving the material recorded in *The Unobstructed Universe*. Later, in seven different seances Joan gave or sent messages to the questioning friend and then one day she came with a carefully worked out statement about certain aspects of consciousness. I refer here only to those comments which bear on the subject of trance mediumship.

To get any picture of the process of trance, Joan said, it needs to be kept in mind that each individual is an energy complex; that is, each individual is made up of a composite of energies mingling in an inconstant pattern which, nevertheless, has a distinct individuality. The physical body is composed of one kind or degree of energy moving at a relatively low rate of vibration, and this pattern of physical energy is itself complex, for the heart, liver, brains and other organs do not have the same frequency; nor are they the same in illness as in health. But there are also other energy patterns which interpenetrate the physical energy pattern; energies characteristic of the emotional and mental aspects of the personality. Psychically gifted persons in all times have frequently been able to see or sense these finer energy patterns as pulsating color. The difference between the physical energy pattern and the emotional and mental patterns is so marked that the psychically endowed often speak of the "mental body" and the "emotional body." It is these finer energies which remain unaffected by death. Although it is often said that "the soul takes off," actually these finer energies simply separate themselves from the physical and remain intact as they have always been.

Attempting an illustration of this intermingling of energies in one individual, Joan advised, "Think of a loose tangle of wire in a general spherical configuration. The tangle has pattern of an intricate sort; geometrical designs intermeshed. Think of the wire as carrying both a magnetic and an electric charge. See both the electricity and the magnetism as moving currents, and let them represent emotional and mental energies. The whole pattern appears alive; it changes shape, sometimes one current outbalancing the other." Here she broke off. "I'm mixing my figure. That's the trouble with an analogy, but I am trying to show you that either the mental or emotional energy may over-produce. The trick is to keep the configuration of personality in balance, of course . . ."

"Now if you think of a larger more open-meshed configuration of wire coming along and opening, as if on a spring, to encompass the smaller more compact configuration of mental-emotional energy, then you have something of an idea of the way in which the physical body takes on, or takes in, the non-physical. Thereafter the strands of energy intermingle—what you know as the physical and the non-physical—and together they form one design, each modifying the other. Really, though, it is fatuous to use such terms as physical and non-physical because both are forms of energy.

"When you raise questions about the mechanics of the trance, bear in mind that while no two persons have exactly the same energy pattern, some are obviously much closer than others. You see the resemblances and differences between physical bodies, and sense the likeness and dissimilarity of certain minds. These variances are a matter of physics, basically, since everything is energy in some form. I am not now going into the self-directiveness of some forms of energy, nor the amenability of some forms of energy to impetus from outside . . .

"Just hold in mind that every individual has an over-all energy pattern, part of which is a distinctive physical pattern and part a distinctive mental pattern. In earth life it is necessary at all times for certain aspects of the mind to maintain some connection with the body because the interplay of mental energy and physical energy operates to a degree in every cell . . . So if the medium's mind wishes to be body-free for any length of time, then some other mind with an energy pattern of about the same frequency, has to cooperate with the medium's body energy. Thus when the medium is in trance his mind is freed for experience in our unobstructed universe, but some discarnate entity is temporarily residenced in his body. Indeed, for the time being the discarnate becomes a living individual in that he inhabits—although not completely—a living body. During trance it is Ford who is 'dead' while his living body is occupied by Fletcher. However, the exchange could not become permanent even if Ford were willing to remain 'dead'."

This line of thought advanced by Joan was contrary to my preconceptions for I had always thought of my mind, for the duration of the trance, as being knocked out, paralyzed, rather than as being free. It was a new idea to me that it is my mind that mingles with the discarnates and impresses their messages upon the body-tending Fletcher who accepts the impressions I give him as his own—as they are in his situation!—and so reports them. Said Joan, "Ford is his own master of ceremonies. He is here with us, on what you call our plane. He feeds his impressions to Fletcher who reports them. However, it is to his own memories that Fletcher has access. Thus he may refer to Acadia as his part of the country or talk about his own religious background. From Ford he gets only such impressions as Ford communicates and they appear to him as his own."

Joan further suggested that we could check these mechanics of the transfer of function. Had we not noticed that if in the midst of a trance session the subject turned to something in which the medium was particularly interested, there was likely to be an expression of the medium's personal views and the source of that expression was usually unidentified or was Fletcher—who strangely had just Ford's views on these particular matters?

Indeed it had often come to me that some points of view and some convictions which I knew to be peculiarly my own occasionally show up in my trance. Said Joan, "On such occasions Ford is just speaking his own piece, taking part in the general discussion and relaying it to Fletcher. And sometimes Ford is so much interested in what is being said here that he goes off with his cronies on this side and lets someone else man the station. There are other discarnate personalities who have approximately his energy pattern and can, if given leave, feed impressions to Fletcher." Thus it is, I presume, that a certain long-winded minister sometimes delivers discourses, occasionally to Fletcher's outspoken disgust.

I am sure there are subtleties in this whole matter of trance communication which we have not yet glimpsed, and it may be we cannot get adequate understanding of the trance—nor of dreams, nor of death—until we probe further into the nature of consciousness, and this may have to wait, in part, for highly trained biologists and psychologists to become trained mediums. Joan has more than once complained that those with whom she now works need mediums "with a vocabulary of ideas as well as of words." She points out that when communication is effected by direct exchange of ideas, symbols can be used to a degree, either as the flashing of a spelled word, or as a picture, but at best symbols are a circumlocution.

"Communication is difficult enough among you in the

physical body. For instance, a poet quotes to a plowman, 'Any man's death diminishes me, because I am involved in mankind,' and the plowman nods, agreeing that all men are related in a vague way. But how much has the poet communicated? In his mind was the lovely figure of the island connected beneath the deep with the continent, and the music of the ensuing lines about the tolling bell, and the personality of John Donne himself, and his times, and his influence on other poets—a hundred connotations which do not exist for the plowman. Now imagine the poet's trying to flash his ideas to the plowman without benefit of words, expecting the plowman to set forth the ideas in poetry. There you have the predicament of communication between my state of consciousness and yours. For us the short of the matter is that if a poet here wishes to impart a poem to someone he loves on earth, he had better send his poem through another poet there among you. And a mathematician here can speak best to and through another mathematician. Concretely, how could Professor Einstein, here with us, discuss modifications of his principle of relativity with a child who has a background of third grade arithmetic—no matter how mediumistic the child might be. We need mediums with well-equipped minds."

Another communicator observed, "Suppose a willing and friendly child who knew both German and English offered his services as an interpreter to Immanuel Kant. No matter how hard each of them tried, the effect on the audience would be less than electric. Another philosopher is needed as interpreter, or at least an educated and urbane humanist."

All in all I may be doing my discarnate friends an injustice in trying to relay what they have tried to say to my sitters through my limited equipment. Here I am limited to reporting what a sitter told me that a discarnate told her . . .

However, on my own authority I can say that clarity of thought has a carry-over from the waking state to the trance state; and that self-interest on the part of a medium tends to obscure transmission of thought from discarnates. Probably even when the best minds are willing to be trained in mediumship there will still remain the need of training in integrity.

Whatever the intricacies of our relationship, Fletcher has become as much a part of my daily life as any of my contemporary friends. I am not dependent upon the trance state for glimpsing his face and knowing that he is at hand. I know him objectively as a personality and the partnership that we effect in trance has made him something of an authority to hundreds of others. People are constantly thanking him—as indeed they should, for without him my effectiveness as a psychic would be greatly limited—and I always feel satisfaction in a tribute to my partner.

The years 1924 to 1927 were the years of our mutual training, Fletcher's and mine. I did an increasing amount of platform work, but always in a tentative fashion. I still did not think of myself as a professional clairvoyant. I wrote articles for various publications under pseudonyms and did some other newspaper and magazine work. On Sundays I frequently spoke in Spiritualist churches, and sometimes in orthodox churches, for my interest in the ministry was ingrained. I gave private sittings and while I always assured my patrons that I could not guarantee Fletcher's appearance, still he nearly always appeared and delivered reliable information, so that I began to make a charge for the sittings. I studied constantly, learning and experiencing as much as possible in the psychic field, and considered these months a time of training, although for what I was not sure. Some day I would go to England and meet the Big Boys in psychic research.

CHAPTER 6

England and the Experts

I WENT TO ENGLAND in the spring of 1927 in a mood of expectation and trepidation. I wanted to meet some of the people who were making history for psychic research, but would my modest gifts interest them? At least I had a letter of introduction to Sir Arthur Conan Doyle and I intended to find a way to present it to him.

At that time Doyle was a household name in America. More accurately, Sherlock Holmes was a household name, and the reason people had flocked to Doyle's American lectures was their desire to see the creator of Holmes and Watson rather than because of any driving interest in survival. Many of them left the lectures, however, with their detective instincts trained on a new area of exploration.

The April day I arrived in London I found that Doyle was to speak that night in Grotrian Hall. Since I knew there would be a crowd, I decided to go down early to find Mrs. St. Clair Stobart who might be willing to give my letter to Sir Arthur. I knew that Mrs. Stobart was one of the most impressive figures in English spiritualism and an active member of the Society for Psychical Research. She was the daughter of an industrialist who had become a baronet, but her own fame stemmed from her war work. At the beginning of World War I she had organized the first mobile hospital unit and accompanied it into Belgium on the heels of the invasion. Captured by the Germans and sentenced to be shot, she managed to escape a few hours before she was to face the firing squad. With her reorganized hospital unit she was then sent to the Eastern Front where she became known as the Lady on the Black Horse. Later she led a section of the Serbian retreat over the mountains to the coast of Greece, bringing out not only a heavy contingent of wounded but also a large number of refugees. For this feat she was decorated by most of the governments of the Western Allies. Back in England, she continued her feminist activities—which had once included being chained to the walls of Parliament, except for breathers, until woman suffrage was recognized. I knew that she was also well established as a writer both of books and of magazine articles. Her friends in America had told me that Mrs. Stobart could always be counted on to have the facts in support of any argument she advanced and that there was no sidetracking her. She was one of the first women in England to get herself onto the vestry of her church.

If I remembered nothing else about that first evening I would remember Mrs. Stobart's striking appearance. Because her life was so busy she could not be bothered about her clothes and had designed a kind of uniform for herself. All of her gowns were made alike, long, but of different materials. This one was of purple velvet. With it she wore flat-heeled shoes with large silver buckles, and a cone-shaped hat atop her abundant disheveled hair. Since she was rather lame and leaned on a heavy stick, some people claimed she looked like a witch. A vigorous and humorous witch, then, and essentially a good-looking woman.

While we waited for Sir Arthur to arrive, Mrs. Stobart

told me about her introduction to things psychic. Right after the war a friend in western Canada had written to ask her to arrange a proxy sitting with a reliable medium. Having no interest in such goings-on herself, she nevertheless went to the best place she knew of, the British College of Psychic Science which provided tested mediums. A transcript was made of the sitting and duly sent to her friend. Later when the friend wrote back to verify most of the message as evidential, Mrs. Stobart's curiosity was aroused, so she attended a series of experiments with Frau Silbert who had been brought to the College of Psychic Science from Graz, Austria, to demonstrate her telekinetic and stigmatic abilities. The demonstration convinced her and she promptly took her stand in behalf of the tenets of spiritualism—which, she said, were merely an underscoring of a forgotten portion of the gospel. It was she and the Rev. Vale Owen, vicar of Oxford, who organized most of the Spiritualist meetings in London. She was a religious person and always differentiated between psychic and spiritual interests. I recall her comment, "Psychism is the science of the seance; spiritualism is the science of the soul."

While we waited for Sir Arthur—I was really quite early—she also invited me to dinner. And that was the beginning of a long and valued friendship. St. Clair ran her houses with her characteristic regard for saving time, hence her weekly menu was the same year around. For years I knew what we would have for dinner on a Tuesday night, say, and that there would be a houseful of people, most of them interesting and many of them distinguished.

When Sir Arthur arrived at the hall we went backstage to meet him. He was a large vigorous man, both simple and commanding in manner. He shook hands heartily, glanced at my letter, and invited me to sit on the platform with him.

So there I was in a choice seat, and no one present was more absorbed in the lecture than I. When Sir Arthur finished, instead of sitting down he quieted the applause and remained standing. Then he said, "We have on the platform tonight a well-known American medium, Arthur Ford." Turning to beam on me, he added, "I am going to ask him to give a public demonstration of his clairvoyant gift."

Instantly I was beyond cerebration, but somehow I walked to the center of the platform. A wave of anxiety swept over me. I felt as if the reputation of American mediumship was at stake. Back home I had always considered my public work an experimental sort of thing, as the audiences in Carnegie Hall well knew. I had never claimed to be a professional medium! I felt myself in a state of shock, but fortunately at that moment I recovered the experimental attitude, and at once felt pleasantly removed from the audience and open toward the spirit world. Everything flowed just right. In the audience, person after person gasped as names were called, details of past experience revealed, comments made upon some present situation for which a departed relative or friend might be expected to have concern. There was some laughter, some tears, and a great deal of interest. When the power waned and I finished, the audience applauded heartily, Sir Arthur beamed again, and St. Clair Stobart took me under her wing.

The following day the *London Express* carried a story by Doyle recounting the occasion. He led off with the handsome remark, "One of the most amazing things I have ever seen in forty-one years of psychic experience was the demonstration of Arthur Ford." Then he gave one incident after another in which he had later checked with the individual for whom some message was intended and found what he considered to be astounding evidence of accuracy. As I read his account, I asked myself how anyone could get all the information that had come through me unless he had invisible friends who were indeed co-operating. Doyle's newspaper story had me convinced!

The following evening Sir Arthur gave a dinner party to which he invited some of his friends, including William Gillette who played Sherlock Holmes on both continents for several years. After the dinner there was a seance and one comment of Fletcher's amused the sitters for years afterward. "Tell my medium to give me more room," he complained. "Last night on that platform—did he expect me to be among the daffodils on the table? I was on his left and he crowded me."

My days were now cut out for me. Shortly after my arrival I spoke at Aeolian Hall and the newspapers again carried a good report. Also at Guilford, a journalist for the *Surrey Times*, present against his own wishes, was sufficiently impressed to write a vivid objective account, including his subsequent checking with various persons who had received messages.

Throughout that stay in England, and on many later occasions, nothing gave me more satisfaction than the time spent with Conan Doyle. He was then a man in his vigorous sixties but he had the zest of a much younger man. When I first knew him I told him how Sherlock Holmes had come into my life back in Florida around 1910 when I found a fine-print copy of *Study in Scarlet* inside the pasteboard container of a bottle of toothache drops. He laughed and said that in 1887 he had sold that tale—the first of his Sherlock Holmes series—to a British publisher for £25 and that he had never received another cent of royalty on it. He said he had patterned Holmes after a professor he had in medical school, a man who was a master of induction. At the time he sold the story he was a struggling doctor in Plymouth, fresh home from a voyage to West Africa, and in need of money to support the household he had established upon his recent marriage.

Doyle was a peerless raconteur and so vivid were his hilarious stories of his medical school days, his early practice, his wildcat investments, his struggle on the Olympic Games committee, his travels in many parts of the world, that I feel to this day that I witnessed many of his exploits firsthand. He had served with a medical unit during the Boer War and had as ghastly experiences as a man could bear to tell. Also in World War I he was out on the British, French and Italian fronts, besides witnessing the final breaking of the Hindenburg Line. His splendid son, Kingsley, whom I knew only from his handsome pictures, had died shortly after the war began. In seances Kingsley often talked with his father and stepmother, Lady Jean. Many people thought it was his son's death which caused Doyle to become a Spiritualist but nothing could be further from the fact.

Doyle's work in the psychic field had begun with telepathy back in the days of his early practice at Southsea. He used to say that as a young medical man he had always compared the thought excretion of the brain to the bile secretion of the liver until he discovered that a friend of his, an architect, could sit some feet behind him and duplicate with a good deal of accuracy anything that Doyle might draw. How could his friend's mind be dependent upon his senses? Then he also found that the friend could do as well across the miles. Was this telepathy? His next experiment was in table-tipping. He set out to prove to a patient of his, a general and a teacher in the Greenwich Naval College, that the general was the victim of hallucination. The result was Doyle's membership in the Society for Psychical Research. However, it was not until he had studied the subject for a quarter century that he accepted survival and communication as facts. Sir Oliver Lodge once told me that when he first met Doyle in 1902 Doyle was willing to admit the possibility of telepathy but would go no further. When I knew him, Doyle liked to quote Sir William Crookes, distinguished physicist and one-time president of the Royal Society, on the subject of survival, "It is incredible but it is true," and he often added a comment made by Baron Reichenbach, a celebrated German naturalist, "There is a scientific incredulity which exceeds in stupidity and obtuseness the clodhopper."

On occasion Doyle liked to hold forth on his conception of sin which had little to do with the frailties of humanity but much to do with the narrowness, bigotry and materialism which he felt to be sins of the spirit. At the same time he did not equate psychic knowledge with salvation, and was always pointing out to spiritualists that many cannibals had psychic power but were man-eaters none the less.

Perhaps the most moving remarks I ever heard him make were on the proclivity of scientists to break the first law of science by pronouncing upon a thing without examination. For me his most unforgettable remark was a comment on the experience of Pentecost as depicted by the author of Acts. "All with one accord," he would quote, and then add that he himself had sat with saintly people and felt the rushing wind, seen the flickering tongues, and heard the great voice, but how could such things happen where harmony in expectation did not reign? Having experienced some of those phenomena myself I would agree with his statement of the prerequisite of harmony.

Both at Crowborough, the Doyle country house, and in their flat in Westminster, I met and sat for many of Sir

Arthur's friends. Hugh Walpole had many sittings both alone and in groups. He was a quiet somewhat dour Englishman with a dry sense of humor. When I first met him he was riding high as the author of his famous horror story *Portrait of a Man with Red Hair* and at work on his series of historical novels. By the time he was knighted a decade later he had come to have a belief in survival—but I do not think the conviction precipitated the knighthood, nor vice versa.

Major Colley, son of Archdeacon Colley, rector of Stockton and ardent in psychic research, was one of the inner circle. There were many majors! With Britain's expansive overseas service there were bound to be a great many retired army and navy men in England and they usually dominated their local society, often being the local tycoon who introduced me at a public meeting. One year my friend Ruby Laffoon, then governor of Kentucky, made me an honorary colonel on his staff. When the news got out in Britain—and it could be that I let it leak out—the majors thereafter scrupulously introduced me as Colonel Ford and accorded me a new deference, even accepting the remarks of my invisible friends as a shade more authentic.

Another of the group around Sir Arthur was David Gow, editor of *Light*, a magazine devoted to psychic research, to which scientists and philosophers alike contributed articles. Doyle used to say that inch for inch he doubted if any other British magazine bore the imprint of as many good English brains. Gow had a fund of firsthand stories of Stainton Moses, the founder and first editor of *Light*. Moses had been a scholarly gentleman of the old school, a minister of the Church of England. His supernormal power had come upon him suddenly, after he had spent much effort proclaiming that spiritualism was spurious and that its showiest exponents, such as D. D. Home, were given to what he called dreary twiddle-twaddle. It was in a seance where he was given a message from a close friend, some years dead, that his dogmatism was shaken. After six months of examination of well-known mediums he began to show signs of great psychic powers himself. This fact interested me because I had noticed that persons who become interested in psychic matters often develop in this fashion, although not to the phenomenal extent of Stainton Moses.

Accustomed as I was to inexplicable phenomena, the tales about Mr. Moses would have left me skeptical had it not been for the caliber of the men who authenticated him. It was through Stainton Moses that the Imperator group gave their teachings from the other side and whether or not they were the distinguished personages they affirmed themselves to be, they were men of unusual stature who would scarcely have worked with, and through, a less cultivated person than Moses.

Along with Conan Doyle one of the most impressive figures I came to know in psychic research in Britain was Sir Oliver Lodge. I first met Sir Oliver at luncheon with Rose Champion de Crespigny, the novelist. Lodge was then a handsome old gentleman in his seventies but as vigorous as many younger men in the Society; he lived to be ninety, I think. Like most great men, he was simple and kindly. He had a lively sense of humor and was fond of telling about certain of his colleagues who had attacked him viciously at one time but had lived to agree that he might not be as mad as they once thought.

Lodge brought to his work in psychic research the same capacity for analysis he had evidenced in his research in physics. In the latter field he was, of course, completely over my head but when he turned to one of his hobbies, such as the dissipation of fog and smoke by electricity—a field in which he had done notable original work—he was as fascinating as a detective rehearsing his exploits. Someone asked Lodge one day in how many learned societies he had served as president; someone else answered for him and the list was impressive, including the long years during which he served as the first Principal of Birmingham University.

Lodge was sometimes irritated at what seemed to him the irrational length to which investigators in the psychic field would go to keep from declaring themselves convinced of survival. In his book *The Survival of Death* he made a caustic observation about the Society for Psychical Research. "It has been called a society for the suppression of facts, for the wholesale imputation of imposture, for the discouragement of the sensitive, and for the repudiation of every revelation of the kind which was said to be pressing itself upon humanity from the regions of light and knowledge." Listening to him, I used to wonder myself if in the final reckoning there might not be as many people embarrassed by their incredulity in the face of evidence as by their overcredulity.

The erudite were inclined to listen to Sir Oliver with respect, if not in agreement, but after the publication of *Raymond,* the common people also listened—if only to argue that "heaven can't be like that." Few books of that day had more sermons preached about them. His son, Raymond, killed in the war, described his initial bewilderment at being dead, his learning to use his new powers and find a new usefulness. Sir Oliver and Lady Lodge went to great pains in setting up what were called cross-correspondences —the fitting together of a coherent message from sentences given to various mediums at approximately the same time or in related sequence.

Anyone who knew Lodge well knew that he was not only a religious man but a churchman. At times he spoke movingly of his religious convictions, and for him there was no conflict between science and religion. "In spite of our ignorance and perplexities," he remarked one day to a group of us, "the outcome of all my studies is the simple but assured conviction that 'the Great Heart of Existence is most wonderfully kind.' "

It was inevitable that a young American medium working with such men as Lodge and Doyle found his days filled with intellectual excitement and personal satisfaction.

In the early thirties Mrs. de Crespigny was Principal of the British College of Psychic Science which worked along lines similar to the older Paris Institute Metaphysique, testing various mediums and making their services available to interested individuals, issuing reports to members, and publishing a scholarly quarterly. The college had been founded a decade earlier by Mr. and Mrs. Hewat McKenzie who brought to it an enormous zeal and a good deal of shrewd common sense so that the work was always of a high caliber. I always felt that Hewat McKenzie, like many men who by their own efforts have achieved a certain amount of success and recognition, was impressed by his own accomplishment. But he had reason to be proud of his college. Mrs. de Crespigny added prestige to everything which bore her name. Her father, Sir Ashley Cooper-Kay, had been First Sea Lord of the Admiralty, and she herself had written a score of popular novels; beside that, she was a beautiful woman, tall, slender, vivacious. Whenever I was in London she was "my girl Rose," and since she was older than my mother at that time I made no bones about my devotion.

It was Mrs. de Crespigny who introduced me to Hannen Swaffer, honorary president of the Spiritualist Union and editor-in-chief of Lord Northcliffe's newspaper empire. Swaffer was affectionately known among newspapermen as "the pope of Fleet Street." In 1924, after Northcliffe's death, when Swaffer heard that the spirit of Northcliffe was reported to have spoken to his former secretary through a medium, he commented that the report was the most ridiculous tale ever circulated. But he smelled a good story. So he went down to the East End to expose this medium. Through the medium a person purporting to be Northcliffe said things of so evidential a nature that he felt no one but Lord Northcliffe could say them, but still he was convinced there was a catch some place. So he went back time and time again to ask questions which he knew only Northcliffe could answer. The evidence became too much for him.

No one who knew Swaffer ever questioned his integrity or his fearlessness, and so the friends who had followed his investigation were not surprised when he took Queen's Hall and told the world that he was convinced that his former chief still lived, remembered, and continued to be interested in newspaper policies. Swaffer then wrote a book, *Northcliffe's Return*, in which he detailed his evidence. We became stanch friends and from Swaffer I learned a lot about dealing with biased and uninformed opponents of things psychic. He taught me to demand that critics come clean with their purported facts about "exposing the medium," producing name and proof of fraud.

One of Swaffer's great friends was Maurice Barbanell who was just starting his career as editor of *Psychic News*. It was he, more than any other, who began to get the data on survival before a wide public, and in his hands data took on excitement. When he heard that some of the staid oldsters thought him a bit sensational, he made the stirring reply, "The truth about survival is the most sensational news in the world." In time Barbanell himself developed remarkable mediumship and was for years the medium for Hannen Swaffer's home study circle, but he kept the fact of his mediumship from the public. The communications of his control, Silver Birch, were known to a vast number of people but it was only in the summer of 1957 that Barbanell finally published his relationship to Silver Birch.

Another of the great British mediums whom I met on my first visit to London was Horace Leaf, one of the oldest mediums in point of service and certainly one of the most reliable and important. I had first learned about him when I picked up a book of his in Roanoke, Virginia, when I was lecturing for Paul Pearson, and right then I wanted to meet him. When I got to London he proved to be a good friend.

In 1928 we arranged between us that Leaf should visit America, take over my work in Carnegie Hall and occupy my apartment, while I went to London and lived in his house. Leaf did a fine job in America and returned for sub-sequent visits.

When I took over his house I found that my first task was to hunt a cook-general, since the woman who had worked for the Leafs did not care to stay on with an American. I also found that Leaf conducted a weekly group at his house attended by thirty to fifty persons. My advertisement for a cook-general appeared in the London *Post* on the morning of the day I was to hold my first meeting. Since it was the first, a really huge crowd came, and about the same time a large number of applicants for the job of cook-general. How to sort the applicants from the guests! Fortunately St. Clair Stobart and Lady Jean Conan Doyle were on hand for the meeting so I impressed them into service to sort the sitters from the cooks. Since they had to explain the situation to all comers, most of the jobseekers wanted to stay for the meeting.

Out of it all I finally got a cook-general who seemed satisfactory to my two experienced friends, and Lady Doyle set the number of pounds per week which the cook was to be paid. She proved most agreeable to my innovations, and when on one warm evening I wanted to serve iced tea she helped me find the ice and then was not at all perturbed when the guests asked to exchange the cold tea for hot. On another occasion she produced delicious southern fried chicken cooked to my specifications but the guests did not care for that either. It was not done that way at that time. That year I entertained a good bit and always marveled at the way this Cockney cook of mine managed to make the weekly budget meet all needs. Eventually I discovered her method. As soon as she heard I was leaving, she herself took off first, whereupon the neighboring tradespeople swarmed in. She had charged everything possible at the stores. I had to cable Francis Fast, in New York, for money to bail me out.

I was fortunate in becoming involved in psychic experimentation when many of those who made psychic history were still working. Although I was too late to meet Professor Crawford of Belfast, I did meet his widow, and also came to know several members of the Goligher circle, especially Kathleen, now Lady Donaldson. Crawford was a lecturer in mechanical engineering at Queens University and his book *Psychic Structures* remains a classic in its field. Through his experiments with telekinetic phenomena he deduced the law of alteration of weights; that is, when a heavy table in the room with a medium was levitated, he found that the increase in her weight was well within 5 per cent of the weight loss of the table; and that sitters bore the rest of the weight loss. Obversely, if a psychic force glued a table to the floor, the medium's weight decreased in proportion to the pressure borne by the floor. During levitation an invisible but palpable substance seemed to stream from the medium's body to act at times as cantilevers. There were other careful elaborations of the experiments carried on under Crawford's trained eye, and I hope some day that a modern physicist will tackle the problem—that is, when he can find an adequate physical medium.

About this time there was an impressive new name at the College of Psychic Science—Eileen Garrett. Mrs. Stobart and Mrs. de Crespigny, as well as Hewat McKenzie, were very much interested in her, both for her good clairvoyance and her trance sittings. Mrs. Garrett has since written of those early days in her autobiography, *Adventures in the Supernormal.* In the spring of 1927 I wanted to consult a good medium in regard to a trip Francis Fast and I were planning to Italy and Egypt, so a friend of mine who had been having weekly sittings with Mrs. Garrett offered to let me keep one of his appointments. She did not know me, nor had I previously seen her, but with her usual graciousness she allowed me to talk with her trance control, Uvani. It was the most amazing sitting I had had up to that time. The people purporting to speak from the other side were my own people who had lived and died in my own country. There could have been no knowledge of them on the part of Mrs. Garrett; nor could telepathy explain the disclosures for she gave me specific details about persons and situations in America of which I myself then knew nothing. For instance, I was told my mother was making a major change and contemplating marriage. This came as a complete surprise to me, for after my father's death she had gone into business with such zest that I supposed her to be a career woman for life. She bought old houses, made them over, and sold them at a fine profit, and she enjoyed her work immensely. Now here was my father, dead more than a decade, speaking to me about going home to advise my mother. The information so upset me that I asked Mrs. Garrett to give a sitting to Francis Fast the next day. He also was urged to go back to the States at once. So impressed were we by these sittings that we canceled our plans and caught the first ship home. Upon arrival we found that the disclosures given through Mrs. Garrett were entirely correct. My mother was about to marry a fine man, Leighton Thomas, who had a plantation in South Carolina. I was delighted with the prospect, helped her to arrange her business affairs, and was grateful not to have missed the wedding.

As I got to know Eileen Garrett better I found that she was as puzzled as I over the nature of mediumship; and as unsure as I that she wanted to be a medium. However, her subsequent career has established her as one of the great mediums of all time and one of the most important people in the field of psychic research. On my second trip to England it was my privilege to arrange a sitting with Mrs. Garrett for Mrs. Helen Bigelow, at that time secretary to the New York section of the ASPR, whose enthusiasm later contributed to bringing Mrs. Garrett to America—a most fortuitous contribution to the cause of psychical research in this country, for out of Mrs. Garrett's work has come the Parapsychology Foundation and the journal *Tomorrow*.

Before I left England, Conan Doyle laid upon my conscience the matter of becoming a professional medium. He felt that both ministers and mediums were called of God, but that since there were more ministers than mediums, I should choose mediumship. Finally I agreed with him and made the decision, but it was a good many years before I understood my calling.

CHAPTER 7

A Round with the Magicians

ONE OF THE MOST passionate exposers of mediums was Houdini, the magician. In the early twenties he threw the entire weight of his reputation as a magician behind his declaration that all mediums were fakes, and that he could duplicate any trick a medium could do.

Although he later played a significant part in providing me with status as a medium, I never met Houdini. He died in 1926 and at that time I was much too inconspicuous to attract his attention. The influence of Houdini upon the whole Spiritualist Movement cannot be understood without some comprehension of the distinction which was Houdini's.

Here was a man who could break out of handcuffs of every invention and contrivance in any part of the world. He could beat the Fiji coin divers at their own game. He staged underwater stunts that astounded the medical profession by the length of time he could hold his breath. He broke out of packing cases built on-stage by local carpenters. Before astonished audiences he caused an elephant (not a rabbit) to disappear and he walked through a brick wall. He was exactly what he called himself, the master magician of his day.

In the early twenties Houdini turned his fabulous tenacity to exposing the whole Spiritualist Movement. There were probably then about a million people in the country who called themselves Spiritualists. In these days when university research in the field of parapsychology has made psychic interests respectable, when extrasensory perception is seriously considered in psychology courses, when the physical scientists are far less dogmatic about the non-physical world than was formerly the case, it is difficult to recover the violent reaction of the orthodox against Spiritualism in Houdini's day. In the orthodox mind all Spiritualists were equated with the lunatic fringe and all mediums were tools of the devil, even if there were no devil. Here Houdini took his stand with the orthodox and lined up his targets.

I have always felt that Houdini was initially honest, even if publicity-minded, in insisting that mediumship, particularly physical mediumship, could be faked. He himself had hoaxed audiences with fake mediumship, and in his mind to be able to trick an audience was to do so. In his early days he had simulated the kind of seance in which material objects are supposed to move by supernormal power, and added assumed authenticity to the act by having himself handcuffed, tied to a chair and placed in a cabinet in such fashion that the audience concurred in his assertion that he could not possibly be the one to set off the tambourine, bell and other paraphernalia on the table in front of the cabinet. Lights went out and the ensuing jingling and knocking were very convincing, as well they might be since Houdini was able to extricate himself from the handcuffs in a matter of seconds, set off his "effects," and relock himself before the lights went on.

Years later, when he was much more widely known, he acknowledged his former fraudulence and developed an act in which he demonstrated the many devices and tricks which he said he had found mediums using. It was after his mother died, however, that he turned to exposing mediums in the big-time manner. It has always seemed to me that he was striking out at people who believed what he himself could not believe—that life goes on. He would leave no one with comfort he could not have. His sentiment for his mother ran deep, even though it often expressed itself melodramatically. There is no doubt but that Houdini informed himself in the field of psychic phenomena, but always from the point of view of looking for the catch. When he read a report based on the testimony of top scientists, he merely averred that they were not as clever as he in seeing through a ruse. He collected a pretentious library, and searched out physical mediums all over the country. Mediums who simply brought through verbal communication were branded liars before he started. He liked to uncover facts upon which to base a story of an exposé but he was not dependent upon facts. As the self-appointed exposer of fraudulent mediumship and ridiculer of Spiritualists, he built himself the biggest reputation in America, and probably in the world.

Nevertheless, that he was at times in touch with genuine communication seems to me certain from opinions I have had from persons who knew him well. I surmise that genuine trance mediums found his antagonistic attitude extremely hard to work with. It is my impression that his mother tried to reach him and could have identified herself if he had been receptive. For instance, Sir Arthur Conan Doyle reported that when he and his wife were traveling in America, Houdini and his wife Beatrice visited them for several days at their hotel in Atlantic City. By that time Lady Doyle herself had developed mediumship and did automatic writing in a semitrance state. Doyle said that on this occasion Houdini received a general message from his mother which moved him greatly, although in spite of his emotion he would not authenticate the message. No doubt it lacked essential words he was waiting for her to say. Eventually Doyle broke with Houdini, accusing him of prejudice and duplicity.

The occasion which brought Houdini into final disrepute with most of the professional research men in the psychic field was an investigation of the famous physical medium Margery, wife of Dr. L. R. G. Crandon, for sixteen years professor of surgery at Harvard University Medical School, conducted by *The Scientific American*. The investigating committee was composed of impeccable scientists and psychologists, including Gardner Murphy, now director of research at Menninger Foundation. Houdini asked to be added to the committee. As the seances continued the committee became increasingly doubtful of Houdini's scrupulosity, not to say impartiality, and made public statement of the fact.

By that time Houdini's reputation was at stake. If distinguished men could prove him wrong in his accusations, the whole country would have a chuckle at his expense, and to be laughed at was one thing he could never accept. Moreover, his enemies the Spiritualists—or so he considered them—would also have a field day. Actually, many Spiritualists had defended Houdini, being more eager than anyone else to have their ranks cleared of frauds.

This was the state of ferment in 1926 when Houdini died, leaving a widely publicized message that if there were anything to the claim for survival he would get through to his wife, Bessie, with a code message which only she could decipher. That this curious last message would have anything to do with my future would have seemed a far-fetched idea at the time.

However, the Houdini virus was contagious and other magicians also broke out in eruptions against spiritualism and mediumship. Among the best known of the magicians was Howard Thurston. Thurston was a tall, suave and handsome man, whom I had always considered a thorough gentleman. Therefore I was surprised when in 1927, the old *New York World* ran a story to the effect that Thurston claimed he had exposed over three hundred mediums, that Spiritualism had broken up more homes than the old-time saloon, and that he had a gadget resembling a watchcase in which was concealed a rubber spook that could be blown up and operated in such fashion that it could duplicate all the phenomena of the seance room. I asked the *World* to let me answer this story, but they refused. There was nothing particularly newsworthy about me. But the United Press Association indicated that they would carry my reply if I made a good story.

Now how could I make a good story of fraudulent accusation of fraud? I thought over the fact that magicians such as Houdini and Thurston kept on issuing open challenges to mediums, offering ten thousand dollars for the production of any stunt they could not reproduce by trickery. I felt there had been about enough of this talk and that someone should make some kind of public refutation which would carry weight. Therefore when a friend of mine, with United Press, suggested that I turn the tables and offer ten thousand dollars to Thurston if he could prove his charges, I was held back only by ten thousand good reasons. Another friend, John Bowman, president of the Bowman Biltmore Hotel Corporation, overheard the suggestion and handed me a certified check. It was posted and I challenged Thurston.

Now the press had a story they could use with relish and they did a thorough coverage. Thurston began to explain to his friends that his press agent had overplayed his hand. But the press demanded a showdown. So a night was set when we were to meet in Carnegie Hall. In spite of the publicity I was surprised to find the Hall packed. Apparently all the magicians were there and the press was amply represented, not to overlook the public.

I spoke first and challenged Thurston, "I will not ask for the names of the three hundred mediums you have exposed, but ask only that you give me the name and address, time, and place of exposure of twenty-five, along with proof that you did expose them." Thurston named only three, none of them living. I could have done better than that. I then asked him to give me the names of only twenty-five families that had been broken up over Spiritualism. He had no names. I could have furnished them, knowing the movement better than he did, for there are always individuals who make a mania of their particular religious beliefs and ride their families to death.

He grew more nervous as we approached the matter of his rubber spook. I explained to the audience the method of testing physical mediumship. However, without these customary preliminaries, I was only going to ask that in good light before the audience Thurston produce this rubber spook and let it walk over to me and tell me the real name of my father. Certainly a kindergarten test for a medium. But Thurston had forgotten to bring the spook along. By that time I felt sorry for him.

The next day the newspapers carried a complete account of the encounter, one paper headlining the story: FORD AND THURSTON PUT ON SHOW AT CARNEGIE HALL . . . IT FLOPPED IN THE SECOND ACT. Thurston explained to the press again that his press agent had got him into this fiasco, hoping to capitalize on the Houdini technique for getting publicity. Reasonably, Thurston's ire was high against me, which I regretted for I admired his magicianship. I supposed our encounter was over.

About four years later I was in Detroit. Thurston had his magical show at a leading theater. I went with a friend. At one point in his routine Thurston did what he called his Spirit Cabinet Trick, and I was surprised to find on the printed program: "This is a trick to amuse you and it is NOT an attack upon the religious beliefs of anyone." When he finished this trick he called for the house lights and had them focused upon me. What next, I thought, deducing that someone had recognized me and told him I was present. Needing revenge, he would embarrass me if he could. Instead, he said to the audience, "What I have just done is a trick, but in the audience is a man whom I firmly believe can help you to communicate with your beloved dead." Then he asked me to come to his dressing room after the show.

When my friend and I went backstage to meet him, Thurston then told me that when we had our encounter in New York he knew very little about psychic things; just what everyone thinks he knows which is usually less than nothing. But he had determined to get back at me so he began sitting with reputable mediums wherever he could find one. "Now as a magician I know the limits of a trick," he said. "Under my own conditions and in my own hotel room I have proofs of survival which satisfy me. I am now a member of the American Society for Psychical Research."

We became good friends and I later attended several seances in his house.

I had no more contact with the magicians, except that I occasionally attended a show, until the evening of February 8, 1928, when a group of friends which included Francis Fast were having a sitting with me. During the trance Fletcher announced that a woman he had not seen before was very eager to say a word. "She tells me that she is the mother of Harry Weiss, known as Houdini." Fletcher appeared very much interested in this person, and began to quote her. Fast took down her message.

"For many years," said Houdini's mother, "my son waited for one word which I was to send back. He always said that if he could get it he would believe. Conditions have now developed in the family which make it necessary for me to get my code word through before he can give his wife the code he arranged with her. If the family acts upon my code word he will be free and able to speak for himself. Mine is the word 'FORGIVE!' Capitalize that and put it in quotation marks. His wife knew the word and no one else in all the world knew it. Ask her if the word which I tried to get back all these years is not 'FORGIVE!' I tried innumerable times to say it to him. Now that he is here with me I am able to get it through. Tonight I give it to you, and Beatrice Houdini will declare it to be true."

When I wakened and the group told me about this extra message which had been slipped in, I was not much interested. Houdini's supposed exposition of mediums had always annoyed me; I thought of him as a wonderful magician with an otherwise bigoted mind and a colossal conceit, and I did not care to have anything to do with him. However, the men at the sitting wanted to give Mrs. Houdini her message. I particularly valued the judgment of Francis Fast, and agreed. Therefore on the following day a copy of the message was taken to Mrs. Houdini. She was completely amazed, and as newspaper files attest, made a public statement over her signature that this was "the sole communication received among thousands up to this time that contained the one secret key-word known only to Houdini, his mother, and myself."

To me she wrote:

67 Payson Avenue
New York City

My dear Mr. Ford,

Today I received a special delivery letter signed by members of the First Spiritualist Church, who testify to a purported message from Houdini's mother, received through you. Strange that the word "forgive" is the word Houdini awaited in vain all his life. It was indeed the message for which he always secretly hoped, and if it had been given him while he was still alive, it would I know, have changed the entire course of his life—but it came too late. Aside from this there are one or two trivial inaccuracies—Houdini's mother called him Ehrich—there was nothing in the message which could be contradicted. I might also say that this is the first message which I have received among thousands which has an appearance of truth.

Sincerely yours,
Beatrice Houdini

That one word "forgive" was not the whole of the mother's message to her daughter-in-law but the rest was of an intimate family nature which concerned Mrs. Houdini and her husband's relatives.

In that first seance the last thing Fletcher had reported about Houdini's mother was simply, "She is going now, and she says that since this message has come through it will open the channel for the other." The other to which she referred was a pact Houdini had made with his wife. He had sworn to get a message through to her if such a thing as survival should prove real. The message was to be based upon a ten-word code which they had used in one of their early shows and which no one but himself and his wife had ever known. The press had given considerable coverage to their agreement. In the months following his death interested persons in various parts of the world were constantly purporting to have received the message from Houdini. And just as regularly Mrs. Houdini disclaimed the messages. It was a poor month when there was no newspaper mention of Houdini and his code.

After the message from Houdini's mother, no further word came for several months. To be sure, no one made any attempt to follow up. Then in November, 1928, the first word of Houdini's own message came through in a sitting for a group of friends, none of whom had known Houdini. The spelling out of the entire message took a portion of eight separate sittings covering a period of two and one-half months. Four of the sittings were with groups of friends and four with individuals, one a New York physician, Dr. John Tanner, and another, Mr. Hamilton Emmons, of England, then visiting in this country.

Fletcher's method was to announce a word as he got it, no matter what else he happened to be talking about, and then apparently to wait until he was sure of another word and make another opportunity. One night he announced, "The first word is ROSABELLE and it is going to unlock the rest." A fortnight later a second word was added—NOW. At a third sitting Fletcher said, "Here is a lady I've been working with for a long time but the only word I get from her tonight is LOOK. This is the sixth word in the code." The sitters presumed that the lady to whom he referred was Houdini's mother. Still later Fletcher asked that four new words be added—ROSABELLE, ANSWER, PRAY and TELL.

At the next to last sitting, Fletcher said, "Let me give you the words from the beginning, because I have to work hard to get them." His last comment was, "This man tells me now that he has put the next five words, which explain these, in French. I have not got them yet. I want to give you the other words because, working on the French words, I may forget the others."

At the final sitting Fletcher said, "This man who is communicating tells me it has taken him three months working out of the confusion to get these words through, and that at no time has he been able to do anything without his mother's help. TELL—that is the last word! You now have ten words. Go over them carefully. It has been a hard job getting them through, 'But I tell you,' he says, fairly shouting, 'they are right!' Now he wants to dictate the exact message you are now to take to his wife. This is to be written down in longhand, no notes."

Fletcher then asked the time, which was 9:23 P.M. He said this was to be noted; also that the medium was in deep trance, that the medium's pulse was at that moment sixty-three, which he asked to have verified; also he wanted the names of those present set down. Fletcher then continued with great exactness, "A man who says he is Harry Houdini, but whose real name was Ehrich Weiss, is here and wishes to send to his wife, Beatrice Houdini, the ten-word code which he agreed to do if it were possible for him to communicate. He says you are to take this message to her and upon acceptance of it, he wishes her to follow out the plan they agreed upon before his passing. This is the code:

"ROSABELLE ** ANSWER ** TELL ** PRAY ** ANSWER ** LOOK ** TELL ** ANSWER ** ANSWER ** TELL.

"He wants this message signed in ink by each one present. He says the code is known only to him and to his wife, and that no one on earth but those two know it. He says there is no danger on that score, and that she must make it public. Announcement must come from her. You are nothing more than agents. He says that when this comes through there will be a veritable storm, that many will seek to destroy her and she will be accused of everything that is not good, but she is honest enough to keep the pact which they repeated over and over before his death. He says, 'I know that she will be happy, because neither of us believed it would be possible.' "

Fletcher then added, "Her husband says that on receipt of this message she must set a time, as soon as possible, when she will sit with this instrument while I, Fletcher, speak to her, and after he has repeated this message to her, she is to return a code to him which will be understood by her and by him alone. The code that will be returned by her will be a supplement to this code, and the two together will spell a word which sums it all up, and that word will be the message which he wants to send back. He refuses to give that word until he gives it to her."

The following day two members of the group, Mr. Fast and Mr. John W. Stafford, associate editor of *The Scientific American*, both strangers to Mrs. Houdini, as were all the members of the group, delivered the message to her. She was lying on a couch, having suffered a fall the week previous. She read the report, then stirred with emotion, dropped it at her side, and said, "It is right!" Then after a moment she asked in wonderment, "Did he say ROSABELLE?" Upon being assured that he had, she exclaimed, "My God! What else did he say?" They repeated all they had recorded.

Following her husband's suggestions, she arranged to have me come to her house the next day, accompanied by three members of the group and a representative of the press. Two of her own friends joined us.

As soon as I was well into trance, Fletcher came through, announcing, "This man is coming now, the same one who came the other night. He tells me to say, 'Hello, Bess, sweetheart,' and he wants to repeat the message and finish it for you. He says the code is one that you used to use in one of your secret mind-reading acts." Then Fletcher repeated the ten words as he said Houdini was giving them to him. "He wants you to tell him whether they are right or not."

Mrs. Houdini replied, "Yes, they are."

"He smiles and says 'Thank you, now I can go on.' He tells you to take off your wedding ring and tell them what ROSABELLE means."

Drawing her left hand from under the cover she took off the ring and holding it before her sang in a small voice:

> *Rosabelle, sweet Rosabelle,*
> *I love you more than I can tell;*
> *O'er me you cast a spell,*
> *I love you, my Rosabelle!*

Fletcher continued, "He says, 'I thank you darling. The first time I heard you sing that song was in our first show together years ago.' "

Mrs. Houdini nodded her head in assent.

"Then there is something he wants me to tell you that no one but his wife knows," Fletcher went on. "He smiles now and shows me a picture and draws the curtains so, or in this manner."

Evidently that was the clue for the unfoldment of the next part of the code, for Mrs. Houdini responded in French, "*Je tire le rideau comme ça.*"

Through Fletcher, Houdini went on, "And now the nine words besides ROSABELLE spell a word in our code." Very exactly he then explained the code. "The second word in our code was ANSWER. *B* is the second letter in the alphabet so ANSWER stands for *B*. The fifth word in the code is TELL, and the fifth letter of the alphabet is *E*. The twelfth letter in the alphabet is *L* and to make up twelve we have to use the first and second words of the code."

Continuing in this intricate way to the end he said, "The message I want to send back to my wife is: 'ROSABELLE, BELIEVE!' "

Fletcher then asked, "Is this right?"

"Yes," answered Mrs. Houdini, with great feeling.

In conclusion Fletcher repeated Houdini's final words. "He says, 'Tell the whole world that Harry Houdini still lives and will prove it a thousand times and more.' He is pretty excited. He says, 'I was perfectly honest and sincere in trying to disprove survival, though I resorted to tricks to prove my point for the simple reason that I did not believe communication was true, but I did no more than seemed justifiable. I am now sincere in sending this through in my desire to undo. Tell all those who lost faith because of my mistake to lay hold again of hope, and to live with the knowledge that life is continuous. That is my message to the world, through my wife and through this instrument."

The code was:

1. Pray	A	6. Please	F
2. Answer	B	7. Speak	G
3. Say	C	8. Quickly	H
4. Now	D	9. Look	I
5. Tell	E	10. Be quick	J

The message itself was:

Answer	B
Tell	E
Pray, answer (1 and 2)	L
Look	I
Tell	E
Answer, answer (2 and 2)	V
Tell	E

The code had been a handy device employed in Houdini's instructions to his wife during their act. Mrs. Houdini commented that the code was such a secret that "even though the stage-hands knew the words, no one except Houdini and myself knew the cipher, or the key, and its application."

From the moment that Mrs. Houdini pronounced the message genuine there began a flood of attack ranging from the ludicrous to the vicious. Mrs. Houdini's veracity was questioned; she was accused of giving the code to someone who then gave it to me—as if there could be any comfort for her in securing a message she already knew from a source she did not believe existed. She was also scored for selling out her own husband who had so widely publicized his conviction that all mediums were fakes. Consistently she avowed the genuineness of the messages and defended having made them public. "It was what he wanted me to do, and I am doing it."

I was likewise accused of fraud, of course, and was once also approached by an ingenious blackmailer. Then a man impersonating me fabricated a newspaper story, which only one tabloid printed, after which he confessed his hoax under promise of immunity from criminal prosecution. Three individuals brought charges to the United Spiritualist League of New York City that I had been in cahoots with Mrs. Houdini and the press. The president of the board of trustees of the First Spiritualist Church redeemed my character, Mrs. Houdini stood her ground, and the respectable press was meticulously fair. I never attempted to collect any of the fabulous sums offered for breaking the Houdini code, although I am sure a legal case could have been made. However, I did receive an enormous amount of publicity. Maybe Houdini had a hand in that! He may have been paying his respects to the fact that my act had been performed not while handcuffed but while sound asleep.

NEW YORK CITY.
JAN. 9TH, 1929.

REGARDLESS OF ANY STATE-
MENTS MADE TO THE CONTRARY,
I WISH TO DECLARE THAT THE
MESSAGE, IN ITS ENTIRETY, AND IN
THE AGREED UPON SEQUENCE,
GIVEN TO ME BY ARTHUR FORD,
IS THE CORRECT MESSAGE PRE-
ARRANGED BETWEEN MR. HOUDINI
AND MYSELF.

Beatrice Houdini

WITNESSED;
Harry R. Zander.
Minnie Chester
John W. Stafford —

Facsimile of statement made by Mrs. Houdini the day after
receipt of the message. Witnesses: Mr. H. R. Zander, Representative of the United Press; Mrs. Minnie Chester, life-long
friend of Mrs. Houdini and Mr. John W. Stafford, Associate
Editor of *Scientific American*.

CHAPTER 8

All in a Day's Work

UP TO WORLD WAR II, lecturing was a routine part of my daily round. Nor have there been many weeks since then when I have not appeared some place, but the planned interview of TV and the radio brings celebrities into the living room, and the trend is toward culture in capsule form, whether the good word is printed or delivered from a platform.

The old-time lecture audience listened to me in a good deal the same attitude they listened to explorers and world travelers. We all spoke of places and dimensions they never expected to visit but they were not going to say such places and experiences did not exist. There was a willingness to be awed and challenged.

During the thirties and forties I spoke to big city audiences and small city audiences. Back and forth across this country and other countries I swung onto trains and stepped out on lecture platforms. And I never lost interest in either the audience or the subject matter. I found I liked pushing back the horizons of people's minds just as much when I did not need the money as when I did.

Besides the general audiences there were specialized audiences composed largely of convinced Spiritualists, many of whom had been members of orthodox churches but felt that the mill-run church led them only to the grave and that if they wanted light for the rest of the journey they would have to turn elsewhere. In New York City quite a gathering of this persuasion met in Carnegie Hall on Sunday evenings. It was to this audience that I spoke for two years, expounding the correspondence between psychic experience and the Bible records, demonstrating communication, and laying on their shoulders responsibility for a life that has endless influence and meaning. The more a psychic exercises his gift the more versatile it becomes, and so the lecture business spiraled.

With the Spiritualists summer is the big season for lectures. Spiritualists still have camps. There was a time when Methodists, Baptists, Disciples and others also held great camps to which hundreds, even thousands, swarmed for a repast of spiritual nutriment. Nowadays most denominations confine their efforts to summer institutes held on campuses, at chartered resorts, or even on their own grounds. But the zeal of the Spiritualists for summer camps has never abated since Lake Pleasant, Massachusetts, began its work in the early eighteen-seventies.

Probably the best-known camp is Lily Dale, situated on an island in Lake Cassadaga, Chautauqua County, New York. Like some of the others it has hotels, motels and cottages for the accommodation of visitors. At Lily Dale some two hundred members own their own homes, and families have come for four or five generations. There is an auditorium which seats twenty-five hundred people and has a splendid pipe organ. Skidmore Memorial Library is housed in a handsome brick building and has thousands of volumes which any psychic investigator is free to use— almost everything in print or out. Recently a healing temple has been built on the grounds and I have watched some remarkable work in spiritual healing. Interests are many-sided at Lily Dale, even including sports.

The Fox cottage, moved from Hydesville, New York, to the grounds at Lily Dale, used to be visited by thousands of persons who looked upon it as a shrine. And since it burned in the early fifties, the plaque which marks the place has become something of a shrine. It was in this little cottage that the two Fox children, Kate and Margaret, first received the rappings which really inaugurated the movement of modern Spiritualism.

In 1846 the Fox family moved into a house in Hydesville in which raps, knocks and noises as of moving furniture soon began to be noted—a good deal as was the case in the John Wesley family a century earlier. Because of the peculiar regularity of the raps, Kate, the youngest daughter, worked out an alphabetical code by snapping her fingers a given number of times. The raps replied in kind. And thus was gradually disclosed a story, the equal of anything in fiction, of the murder of a peddler.

After the family and neighbors had been drawn in on the communications which came by way of the rappings, scores of prominent persons visited the Fox cottage, and their ensuing dwellings, to investigate. Time and some genuine scholarship have brought the broad outlines of the Fox phenomena into focus.

Spiritualists believe that the modern Spiritualist movement was instigated by an organized effort on the part of discarnate church members, still ardent in their devotion to the Church Universal, to bring back into the thinking of religious people some of the forgotten truths upon which the church was founded. Spiritualists also call attention to the fact that the modern movement sprang up almost simultaneously with the publication of Darwin's theory of the origin of species. Just as Darwin furnished scientific impetus to mankind to move out of a static universe into an evolving vital universe, so the founders of Spiritualism extended the idea of the universe to include the continuing development of the soul after death. They felt the case was clear for survival and there should be further investigation of the nature of this larger dimension of consciousness. Either man survives death or he does not, they insisted; it is an either/or proposition. Moreover, it is a proposition of such enormous significance that it demands universal attention.

The people who now attend the camps are a cross section of American life. Some are professional persons— lawyers, doctors, ministers of orthodox churches, teachers, musicians, scientists; more are businessmen and housewives. The whole economic scale is there and the entire social spread. Most of the young people, of whom there are many, have grown up in Spiritualist homes and have been taught in the Lyceums, which in Spiritualist nomenclature means Sunday Schools. There are also many old people. For the most part, Spiritualists are a healthy, sane and happy lot; not the lonely grief-stricken people that the uninitiated often imagine.

But there are some queer ones at a Spiritualist camp! In what religious groups are there not some off-center individuals, some cheerful riders of splayfooted hobbyhorses. Some Spiritualists project themselves into the higher worlds before they have learned to live in this world, becoming completely engrossed in their immortal span before they know what to do with themselves on a rainy afternoon. Or they may develop a bizarre routine for hastening psychic unfoldment.

I recall a stout woman who did calisthenics by the lake every morning and then made the rounds from cottage to cottage blowing soap bubbles to drive out the devils. There was a man who called himself a lycanthropist: he could tell by looking at an animal what human individual might temporarily be using that animal's body. Thus a pet cat having a fit was being used by Aunt Sally in a temper tantrum, or a cow lowing mournfully was Uncle Eben calling his departed soulmate. He had amassed some astounding data. For instance, a shot fired by an avid African hunter might ostensibly kill only a hyena but in a neighboring village the witchdoctor might die at that very minute, which showed that the witchdoctor had been temporarily indwelling the hyena for the purpose of absorbing its energy and cunning. There is a literature on the subject of lycanthropy, some of which engaged the attention, but not the corroboration, of Sir James G. Frazer when he was compiling *The Golden Bough*. Then there was the woman who could eat no "dead" food; she had to see the living aura of a vegetable which meant it could be no more than ten minutes from its garden home. She caused her faithful daughter a deal of trouble in winter. Perhaps these oddities at a camp, as elsewhere, serve as deterrents to those who tend to ride one horse to death.

At Lily Dale, as at most of the better camps, the program is built around the featured speakers. The week opens with a Sunday afternoon lecture by the leading speaker, followed by a public demonstration of clairvoyant communication. On such occasions I have sometimes spoken to thousands of people. Then throughout the ensuing week further lectures are followed by further demonstrations. There are also daily classes for the serious-minded, dealing with the philosophic, scientific and religious aspects of Spiritualism. In various camps I have conducted classes numbering as many as five hundred. Seminars for training psychic gifts or for training in leadership are smaller. Plenty of time is left for investigators, or anyone else for that matter, to sit privately or in groups with mediums who are properly certified by the camp authorities. The program does not vary greatly in plan in the twenty-five or more camps.

Contrary to the popular idea that Spiritualists are lax and unconcerned about the qualifications of mediums, the reputable organizations are more concerned with keeping their ranks clean than any outsider could be. They know that all mediumship is questionable in the minds of the uninformed, but more important—a fraudulent medium is of no real use to a Spiritualist. Moreover, Spiritualists are more canny, because more experienced, in detecting fraud than many psychic investigators. A fake medium may appear on the scene with an impressive bag of tricks, but I never knew one to last long.

Authentic mediums are not likely to attend the same camp for more than two or three years in succession because, try as they may, it is impossible to keep from getting to know the people who attend habitually, and as soon as a medium knows his audience then his offerings are suspect. Personally, I feel strongly that the only value of public demonstration of psychical phenomena of any sort lies in its evidential nature. Therefore I protect myself by not returning to the same camp for a period of time.

For many years I have considered myself a part of the Spiritualist movement. This does not mean that I ever lost my feeling of identity with my own brotherhood, known as the Christian Church or Disciples of Christ, nor that I have ever wanted to separate myself from the main stream of Protestantism. Moreover, the concerns of Spiritualism have never been my only religious concerns, but I feel that the gospel is truncated when it does not proclaim the resurrection of Jesus and the immortality of the soul. Hence much of my work has been done with those who do so believe.

Only once have I come to issue with the Spiritualists'

national organization and that was over a matter that would never be raised in these days. Many years ago an opinionated gentleman with a marked racial bias got himself into a position of national leadership and used such authority as he had, augmented by the pressure of like-minded friends, to move against the membership of Negroes. Along with other leaders of the New York State delegation, I made a strong stand for an interracial fellowship. The altercation was taken to a national meeting and for a time we lost, but before long popular sentiment supported us and the question was settled once and for all. Not many denominations came to this stand as quickly and unequivocally. Today the Spiritualist movement is both interracial and international.

On the Spiritualist position, many Spiritualists feel that "he who is not against us is with us," for many members of orthodox churches share the basic tenets of Spiritualism. And it is also true that hundreds of members of Spiritualist churches share some of the other concerns of Protestantism which Spiritualist churches are inclined to overlook. One day the yeast will leaven the lump but which is yeast and which is lump will take some time to determine.

While taking an active part in the Spiritualist movement I have also participated in the services of a good many other Protestant churches. In the winter of 1934–35, for instance, I spoke on Sunday evenings in the Church of the Divine Paternity. This is the Universalist church of which Joseph Fort Newton became pastor after he left the great Methodist City Temple of London. Dr. Charles Francis Potter had preceded Dr. Newton at Divine Paternity and I had heard him lecture at Lily Dale, where many outstanding ministers preached in the summer. After Dr. Newton left his New York pulpit to assume the pastorship of the St. Paul's Episcopal Church in Overbrook, suburban

Philadelphia, Dr. Frank Oliver Hall, pastor emeritus, officiated at the morning services of Divine Paternity. One night a parishioner of Dr. Hall's brought him to hear me at Carnegie Hall and Dr. Hall saw so many of his flock in the audience that he decided they ought to be able to hear the kind of gospel they wanted to hear in their own home church. Hence the invitation to me. The church was always crowded and the audience as appreciative as any I remember. I felt that our association was mutually profitable. That winter's preaching at Divine Paternity is the nearest I have come to having a pastorate since I left Kentucky, but I have continued to speak at individual services of other denominations.

Sometimes a sermon has a different outcome than the one intended. At the earnest behest of a friend of mine I spoke one night in an underprivileged section of New York to a rapt and sizable audience. On any occasion the audience has as much to do with the effectiveness of the service as does the speaker but on this occasion the empathy of the audience was terrific; they seemed to anticipate my words. I noted, however, that their nodded approval, and even their amens, came at the most unexpected times. When I recapitulated, "Twelve apostles, five thousand people, three loaves and five fishes, one Lord," they all but left their seats. Later in the week when I saw the minister of the church he was grinning ear to ear. Almost every member of his church, he said, had "played the numbers" upon which I had dwelt in my sermon; his wife had got a new refrigerator with her earnings and one woman had made two thousand dollars.

Symposia and panel presentations have always interested me. I remember particularly a meeting in the Emil G. Hirsch Center of Sinai Temple, Chicago, back in 1934. Rev. James M. Gray of Moody Bible Institute spoke on the topic "Is Death the End?" presenting the tenets of fundamentalism. He was followed by Dr. Charles W. Gilkey, dean of the University of Chicago Chapel, who gave a scholarly address on immortality as an adventure in faith. Professor Arthur H. Compton who had recently won a Nobel prize in physics spoke on certain scientific trends which gave belief in immortality a strong position as a scientific possibility. I spoke simply of what I had heard and seen—which included the duplication of a great many of the miracles recorded in the Bible.

As I look back over hundreds of public meetings I am surprised at the number of friends I have made through some individual's response to a talk. For instance, Will and Alice Turner. Dr. Turner is now a consulting chemist for various government and private agencies, but back then he was on the faculty of the University of Missouri, and before that an associate professor at the University of Chicago, from which school he had secured his doctorate. While on sabbatical leave, the Turners came to New York and having a mild interest in survival they hunted out the services of some Spiritualist Churches, including a meeting at which I was speaking. They tell me that in a period of open clairvoyance, I announced the presence of Dr. Turner's father and uncle, giving their names as Fletcher gave them to me, and also the presence of Alice's mother who requested that they search out her brother Charles of whom they had lost track. The mother held up a young child, said Fletcher, and assured them she was caring for it. Unknown to anyone near them, for they were strangers in New York, they had lost a two-year-old child the previous year. They asked Fletcher whether they were likely to stay in New York, and the mother answered yes, they would stay. And such proved to be the case. Later they also located the brother, Charles, and at a propitious

time, for he was suffering from a severe automobile accident. And from that incident stemmed our continuing
friendship.

Sometimes at public meetings it is by inadvertent usefulness to a stranger that I make a friend. One night in the
late thirties Ralph Harrison, now a clairvoyant of no small
ability himself, came to hear me at Carnegie Hall. At that
time he was unknown to me; just another member of the
audience. Nor did he put much stock in the disclosures of
mediums. He had just enough curiosity to accompany his
mother to the meeting and that was all. During the messages
at the close of the talk, I asked (I am told), "Is there a
Ralph . . . Ralph . . . Ralph Harrison present?" Harrison
acknowledged his presence. Whereupon I told him that,
according to Fletcher, he must have something to do with
banks or banking, and he said that he did. I continued, "I
am told to warn you to be careful when going to the bank.
You must carry considerable sums of money with you and
you must take precautions or there is likely to be a hold-up.
See?"

Mr. Harrison thanked me for the advice—and went on
taking the daily bank deposits of thousands of dollars from
the Newark firm of the Kreuger Brewing Company, of
which he was credit manager, to the nearby bank in his
own car, without armed escort. In less than three weeks
after my warning, Harrison was held up by two armed
gunmen who seized his day's deposit and made off in a
car. May I say that Harrison became a friend of Fletcher's
forthwith and that his interest in psychic affairs was sharply
whetted?

Another night, after speaking to an immense audience
at a Spiritualist meeting in New York City, I mentioned
that there was a message for a woman named Ethel. Several
hands went up. I looked them over and pointed to a hand-

somely dressed woman near the front at my right. "The message is for you. It comes not from one man but from three men." Then I described the three. "They are standing in a row with their hands across each other's shoulders. They want you to know what good friends they are, and each one wants you to know that he loves you very much. They feel that this message is important to you, especially the fact that they are such good friends."

Later I found that this woman was a complete disbeliever in the possibility of communication but she had come to the meeting with a friend. She was very much a society woman and she had had three wealthy husbands, all of whom had died. She had always worried over the fact that she had three husbands in heaven and was afraid that when she arrived among them they might quarrel over her. Her relief was enormous to feel assured they were friends and all still cared for her. Whenever she speaks of the wonderful meeting in New York I know she is thinking of that one short message.

CHAPTER 9

Tried and Tested

As OFTEN AS POSSIBLE I went to South Carolina to visit my mother and my stepfather. Life was gracious in their household and meals were well served. I was surprised, therefore, when I came down to breakfast on the first morning of a visit, to find the new maid standing as far from me as possible when holding a serving dish; then to see her remain standing beside my mother while she shoved the biscuits half the length of the table to me.

My mother looked amazed, frowned, and finally turned to Euphronia, raised an eyebrow and asked, "Euphronia, *why?*"

Euphronia knew the answer. "Because I ain't gettin' too near anybody's got ghostes followin' them around."

Euphronia spoke for those persons in various walks of life who are afraid, or at least half-afraid, of anyone who has touch with the dead. To be afraid of a medium as the mouthpiece of a discarnate is about as sensible as falling into an ague because unseen persons speak on the radio.

Even more common than fear is suspicion. I am suspected of trying to make people have faith! Many people feel that the best news must be false merely because "it's too good to be true." If the dead live, then death *has* indeed lost its sting, a condition devoutly to be hoped for but not believed in. They feel I am trying to force them to believe. Besides our generation is accustomed to being told *how* things work; not that the average one of us understands the how of television, diesel engines or jet propulsion but we like to know someone else understands. I am suspected of chicanery somewhere because I cannot explain how I am doing what I am doing—and I cannot, although I am prepared to explain more than they are usually prepared to take in.

Professional investigators, on the other hand, tend toward the theory that the medium is probably honest but self-deceived; he has picked up information which he stores in his subconscious mind—by whatever name they call it—and he deals it out under hypnotic suggestion. Their only hope of acquiring untainted messages is to eliminate every possible source through which the medium could obtain access to the particular bit of information they consider veridical; the medium would cheat if he could and hence must be protected from himself.

Now it does something to a man's nature to live constantly surrounded by suspicion. Professional mediums are likely to be lonely persons. In a friendly gathering they grow afraid to be friendly lest inadvertently they pick up information about their acquaintances which later will come out in a seance and vitiate the evidential. One wonders that mediums are ever normal persons, set apart and suspected as they are. Just the same, some of my best friends have come into my life first as doubters. A recent letter from Upton Sinclair brought to mind our first encounter.

Sinclair first came to me for a sitting in 1930, accompanied by his wife and Professor William McDougall, then of the Harvard University Department of Psychology. One of the tests the three of them had rigged up was based upon five letters selected from Sinclair's files, all written by persons who had died. I was told nothing of the letters nor of the nature of the test when they came, and within a few minutes after their arrival I was in trance. Later, when Sinclair sent me the report he was publishing, I found that the letters were from Eugene Debs, labor leader, socialist, and close friend of his; Jack London, writer, and a treasured friend; Conan Doyle; George Brandes, the Danish critic; the other I did not recognize. Sinclair wrapped each letter in a large sheet of green paper and put each one into a separate brown manila envelope. Mrs. Sinclair and Professor McDougall inspected the envelopes. Sinclair reported that during the trance Fletcher described Jack London and gave them several messages from him, ending with London's remark, "You have a letter of mine here." Fletcher asked Sinclair if that was true and when Sinclair acknowledged that it was, Fletcher asked that the letter be handed the sleeping medium, after which Fletcher commented further on its contents. In the same way, the medium held the other letters and promptly produced their writers, so to speak, who entered into the common discussion. The comments from Debs, who had written his letter in prison, were very moving; he was a simple man who wanted to help this weary world.

Sir William Osler was one of those who spoke especially to Professor McDougall, offering various bits of evidence, none more convincing to McDougall—to whatever degree he was convinced—than his remarks about his former attitude toward phenomena undemonstrable by the scientific method. "I have talked with G—— [he named a colleague who had been interested in psychic affairs] in this world," said Osler. "On earth I wouldn't have talked with him. I wouldn't have bothered." Fletcher's last comment on Osler was, "He says to tell you, when you go through his workshop, to just lift your hat and he'll see you."

The pains to which a sound researcher will go to check the smallest details never fail to impress me. Fletcher gave the first names of both McDougall's mother and father, describing both and giving messages from them. The following day, meticulous McDougall raised the question as to whether, since I had had two days' notice of the sitting, I might not have looked up his forebears in the encyclopedia. Whereupon Sinclair, out-carefulling McDougall, went to the library to check, but could not locate the first names of McDougall's parents. *Who's Who in America* gave the initials while the British *Who's Who* had nothing. Sinclair examined every edition of *Who's Who* back to 1913 and then asked two reference librarians in Los Angeles and Pasadena to search, which they did, through encyclopedias, magazine articles, and books. They found no mention of McDougall's parents' first names. Moreover, their names were uncommon names, a fact which gave Sinclair some satisfaction. As it did me!

Professor McDougall's restrained comment on those Sinclair sittings was summarized in a sentence, "Through Arthur Ford I have witnessed genuine supernormal mental phenomena."

In one of Sinclair's later sittings a message was sent by a discarnate girl, who said she had died very young, to a woman she said was her mother. Sinclair was certain that this woman, a friend of his, had never had a daughter. When he told her of the message the woman forthwith burst into tears. She had had an abortion, she said, and the name by which the spirit child identified herself was the name the mother had called her in the prenatal months. Sinclair used this story in his long novel *Between Two Worlds*. Recently a friend of mine told me that she wanted to find that story and decided to read through the book until she came upon it. The book has 855 pages and she found the story on page 844. She said she wished she had consulted Fletcher about that page number.

In the same novel Sinclair told the story of Sir Basil Zarahoff, using other names. I met Sir Basil through Lady Zoe Caillard, the widow of Sir Vincent Caillard who had been a director of Vickers-Armstrong munition works. Sir Basil was a small, tight-lipped man, always tense and highly nervous. He was often called "the mystery man of Europe"; some said he was Greek, some Turkish, and many held that he was the richest man in the world. If so, his riches bought him small happiness for his one personal interest seemed to be his wife and she lived only about three years after their long-deferred marriage. After his wife's death Lady Caillard persuaded Sir Basil to try to communicate with her and brought him to me. His relief in proving to his own satisfaction that she lived afforded him a late but transforming kind of happiness. In the Sinclair novels he made the medium a woman and gave her a Polish name but the data are factual.

When Sinclair published his book *Mental Radio* he had enormous pleasure in Albert Einstein's written comment, "In no case should the psychologically interested pass over this book without heed." Sinclair felt that his meticulous methodology and his insistence upon letting his facts make their own point had paid off.

Lewis Browne, author of *This Believing World* and many other books, was one of Sinclair's group. He was frightened and antagonistic and ridiculed everything psychic until he had an experience, through Fletcher, of having his mother refer to a watch she had given to him, and particularly to an inscription upon it, the meaning of which only she and he knew. Then he was shocked to attention and to a degree of open-mindedness. His friend, Theodore Dreiser, freely attested the findings of their experimental sittings with me.

One of the more indefatigable researchers who came to me in my earlier years in New York was Florizel von Reuter. At the time I knew nothing about him but he had been a boy wonder violinist, giving command performances for Queen Alexandra and Edward VII, and for the Sultan of Turkey with his two hundred wives; and in adulthood he continued to be a top violinist. Conan Doyle knew him well and had particular admiration for his ingenious and painstaking methods of testing psychic manifestations. But in 1926 when Reuter first came to me I had not yet met Doyle.

I think it was Dr. Walter Prince, then research officer of the American Society for Psychical Research, who suggested to Reuter that he see me. I knew nothing about Reuter's personal affairs, nor where he made his home and certainly did not understand the Italian language in which he sometimes spoke to his communicators.

In the course of my trance Fletcher announced that there was a man on his side who wished to send a message to his own mother. "The name he gives sounds something like Gebart and he says his mother used to live in the same place that Reuter lives." Fletcher went on that the man said he used to be a postman or messenger and bring letters and telegrams to Reuter. Neither Reuter nor his mother could remember any such person and asked the name of the town. According to Reuter's notes, Fletcher answered, "It is a place with a name, as I understand, something like 'Vicksburg'—no, that is not right—wait, I'll get it. Weis—Weissen—yes, that's it, Weissenburg." He spoke the name as it sounds in German—Vīs′en·boork. This was indeed the name of a German town in which Reuter spent most of his spare time. Fletcher continued, "He says he died during the war in a hospital in Coblenz. His mother does not live in Weissenburg, but some relatives of his used to live in a house which you reach from where you live by going three blocks to the left of the gateway, and then two blocks to the right."

Reuter then realized that the description fit a house in which an old woman named Gebbers used to live, but he knew nothing about her or her family. "The old lady you knew is not his mother," said Fletcher, "but some relatives used to live there."

Reuter kept his notes, unlikely though it seemed to him then that he could be getting evidential messages from across the ocean. The next June when he returned to Weissenburg Castle, he made inquiries of the Princess Victoria, who knew the village well, and also of the villagers, but the old woman Gebbers had moved away several years previous and no one knew anything about her or the present situation of her relatives, although all felt sure she had never had a relative killed in the war. However, a few weeks later old Mrs. Gebbers came back to Weissenburg village on a visit and called to see the Princess. The Princess asked her if she had lost any relatives in the war. "Oh, yes, I lost a nephew; that is, a nephew of my husband. He died in a hospital of a wound. He used to be one of the postmen here—don't you remember?"

At this same sitting Fletcher brought through a Swiss lady whom he described and named Mrs. Honegger. She had been a dear friend of Reuter's but she had died some five years previous. He spoke to her in Swiss dialect, to which Fletcher responded in English and said she was talking about someone to whom she referred as "Girlie" or "young Girlie," as nearly as he could make out. Reuter knew that Frau Honegger's pet name for one of her daughters was "Yug-gerli," and so asked about her. The mother reported that she had had some clothes stolen and that they could be found at a house in the suburbs on the river. When asked the address where her daughters lived, she got through the number but had a time with the name Zurichbergstrasse, getting the middle syllable *berg* first. A few weeks later Reuter located the sisters at that address and found the story of the stolen clothes to be correct.

On another occasion Reuter received, via Fletcher, a message which he considered even more evidential than discussion of matters which are verifiable because it established the character and personality of the unseen communicator. A man who gave his name as Nicolò and was described by Fletcher as Paganini, first established himself with the comment that Reuter had not practiced enough that day—a fact to which Reuter agreed. Then Paganini proceeded to give him advice about not playing Bach at that time to the American public. When Reuter asked about using the Tschaikowsky Concerto as the principal number on his program, Paganini acquiesced but added that he would like to go over the whole program with him. Furthermore, he remarked, he thought that at the last concert the accompanist had played too loud in the final movement of the concerto—the long passage in double harmonics. Reuter then asked what Paganini thought of the teaching method of a certain violinist in Berlin who claimed that he had discovered the secret of Paganini's way of holding his bow. At this point, Reuter told me later, I sat up in my reclining chair—still in trance of course—and Fletcher spoke with great vigor. "He says, Imposter! He says for you to look at a picture of him, in Florence, which gives the exact position of his violin."

For the record, I had not attended Reuter's concert in New York and had no idea how the accompanist had played; nor do I know one thing about violin music. Some years later I met Reuter in London and we had sittings both in Doyle's home and in Reuter's apartment. At one sitting, attended by a score of important personages, Fletcher brought through a variety of messages, so that everyone present received something which he felt evidential—a most unusual circumstance. I confess I was impressed by Fletcher's clarity when I saw the transcript of that evening's work.

Still later in Germany I stayed with Reuter and his mother for several weeks at the castle of their friend and patroness, Princess Victoria Reuss, a cousin of the Hohenzollerns, Germany's last royalty. Reuter's discarnate friends seemed co-operative in producing intricacies for his investigation, for just as he had received messages in America regarding acquaintances in Germany, so now in Germany he received messages regarding persons in America. There were several detailed messages purporting to come from Reuter's first music teacher in Iowa. For verification the messages had to be sent to a sister of the communicator, then living in California. Later Reuter published some of these experiences with me in his book *Psychical Experiences of a Musician*. Bozzano, dean of Italian researchers, felt that some of Reuter's investigations were among the most evidential of recent times. Through the years Reuter and I have continued to meet at intervals, and his zest for psychic investigation is unabated.

It was at the Fulton Oursler home that I met Dr. Nandor Fodor, now a practicing psychoanalyst in New York City and the author of the compendium of psychic data, *Encyclopaedia of Psychic Science*. In the twenties he was new in America and a very skeptical investigator indeed, persuaded to participation only by Oursler's hardheaded persistence. The first sitting Fodor ever attempted

was at my place in 1926. However, I was not the medium
for this seance. It was William Cartheuser, a direct voice
medium who was sitting under strict test conditions. Oursler published an account of that seance and branded the
medium a fraud. He stated that the seance was held at my
house, mentioned that the medium had a harelip, insisted
he was a fake, but neglected to say that I was not the
medium. The article was signed by the name Samri Frikell,
one of Oursler's many pseudonyms. When I read the
report I was in California and I wrote to him, "I don't
mind being called a fake for I'm used to that, but I do not
happen to have a harelip." I received an amusing apology
from Oursler. He and his wife, Grace Perkins, a novelist,
were my good friends for years. Even after he became a
convert to Roman Catholicism we continued to discuss our
mutual interest, for he was a member of the board of a
spiritual healing group which restored me to health after
my physicians lost hope for my recovery.

Most tests are carefully planned and supervised but occasionally an inadvertent disclosure becomes proof of
authenticity. Once I spoke to a sizable audience in the
Hotel Statler ballroom in Cleveland and gave a message to
a young man in the audience from a discarnate who said
that he was the man's father. After the meeting the younger
man came up to me with an older man and said, "You made
one mistake tonight, Mr. Ford. The 'spirit' who sent me
the message was not my father. My father is right here
with me"—and he introduced the older man by his side.
Then the older man rather gulped, took a deep breath,
shook his head and said to the younger man, "You were
not born my son; you are my adopted son. I believe that
was your real father who sent you the message and it's
better for all of us to get this straight."

Occasionally tests are proposed in the press. I recall,

for instance, the writer of a gossip column who wrote in his column, "Ford says he has spoken with Houdini, but I challenge him to produce Isaiah." I told him I might promise to produce Isaiah if he would promise to prove that the man I produced was or was not Isaiah. Who would understand Isaiah if he spoke in his ancient Hebrew tongue? Or check his authenticity if Fletcher interpreted in English? Certainly not the columnist. On the other hand, a man can test out his grandmother, his brother, sister, or any close friend by scores of small matters known to the two of them.

One test of validity in communication stays in my mind not because the people involved were famous, although some of them were, nor because they went to considerable trouble and expense to carry through their test conditions, although they did, but because the conditions themselves were so unusual. I was not the medium involved. In this case I was one of the experimenters.

In the late twenties when a reporter named Goldstrom from a Washington paper was interviewing Conan Doyle, the talk turned on aviation and the reporter asked Doyle what effect, if any, height and speed might have upon psychic phenomena. Conan Doyle's reply was a question, "Why not go up in a plane and make the experiment?"

A dozen years passed; Doyle died, and Goldstrom became aviation reporter for a chain of American newspapers. During that time his interest in psychic matters had deepened until he knew a good deal about mediumship. One day he came to me and asked if I would coöperate with him in a test he wanted to make under special conditions. He wanted to hire a plane, take a small group of interested friends and a medium, fly above the tumult of the city and see what sort of contact we might make with someone who would be well known to the group. I told him I would be much interested. Then he wanted to know if I knew a medium capable of bringing through, or producing, the direct audible voice of a discarnate. There are such mediums. I do not understand the psychophysiological process upon which they work or are worked upon, but I have heard them produce the direct voice of a given discarnate and I have recognized the voice as unmistakably as ever I could have known it when the individual was living. After considerable consultation, we decided to invite Maina Tafe, who was the medium through whom the artist Bessie Clark Drouet received help, and Miss Tafe agreed to experiment with us.

Our second task was to decide upon the passengers for the trip. We decided to include Dr. David Henry Webster, a distinguished surgeon at Manhattan Eye, Ear and Throat Hospital; Mrs. Rita Olcott, widow of Chauncey Olcott, the famous Irish tenor, who was known as one thoroughly grounded in knowledge of mediumship; Everett Britz, one of the leaders of the Fusion party which had helped to bring Mayor La Guardia into the New York City government, and who was also treasurer of the General Assembly of Spiritualists in America; Jacob Padawer, who would know how to deal with unfair reports from the sensational press; and Princess Rospligiossi, an intimate friend of Conan Doyle's who would recognize his voice as readily as I would myself. It was Doyle's voice we especially hoped to hear.

The third task was to hire a plane and pilot. It seems amazing that any pilot should have hesitated to man the venture but several refused to have anything to do with a plane full of people who intended talking to the dead! Finally one was engaged to take us up on a transcontinental plane for an hour's flight.

Our only special preparation was securing heavy paper

over the windows to shut out the light. Mediums who produce physical phenomena seem to work better in the semi-dark, for what reason I do not know, but I suspect that the fact that radio also seems to come in clearer at night has some bearing on the matter.

We settled into our places and the plane rose at once to something over eight thousand feet. The vibration shook loose the paper, which we had fastened rather casually, and brilliant moonlight as well as light from the wings flooded the cabin. The psychic's hands were held by two of the passengers and obviously she had no paraphernalia.

Suddenly a voice was heard by all present—Conan Doyle's voice. Anyone who had ever heard Sir Arthur would know that voice for his, unmistakably. He reminded Goldstrom of their discussion and spoke of many things of an intimate nature, familiar only to the passengers who had known him well.

Other voices broke into the conversation. Dr. Webster's son, who had recently died in Vienna, spoke to his father. Then a voice purporting to be that of Floyd Bennett, one of the great early fliers of this country, spoke out. "You are now directly over the airfield named for me." Since we had given the pilot instructions to fly up the Jersey coast, circle west and return to the airport, we felt that the intruding voice was mistaken. The passenger nearest the pilot room opened the door and asked the pilot where we were. His answer was, "Centered over Floyd Bennett Airfield." He had found flying conditions such that he had decided to change our course.

Other discarnates spoke. From one end of the plane to the other voices of persons who were supposed to be safely buried in England and Austria and various parts of America all spoke in their individual and distinctive tones and cadences and were recognized by those who were in a position to recognize them. Some of their comments were too tender and heart-searching to be reported, even now, after the years have passed.

When the medium wakened, all those present knew not only through objective experience but with the inward awareness of a man who seeks truth that for a fleeting starry hour we had ridden in a world of beauty and understanding love where neither death nor distance are barriers. Moreover, we found that the higher we got above the spiritually murky atmosphere which hangs like a pall over a modern city, the clearer was our perception.

When we returned to earth I noted about my fellow passengers a strange detached air. One does not come back from so far a place unchanged.

CHAPTER 10

The People Who Come

MOST PEOPLE who come to me do not come in order to test me out but simply because they want to get in touch with someone whom they have, as we say, "lost." They want the one who has gone on to know that he or she is still loved, missed and treasured; and they want the one who has passed from sight to give them assurance of continuing existence and love. This is what they want even though they do not actually believe it is possible to communicate.

Some come in open grief. I like to greet them, put them at their ease, tell them what to expect, and then get myself out of the picture by going right into trance. Usually the discarnate they are seeking will talk with them through Fletcher, evidencing enough intimate knowledge so that they are touched if not completely convinced. Or rather, they are convinced while the trance is in session, but later, after they have gone home and discussed the experience, doubt begins to fill the mind. People cannot believe anything that does not "make sense" within the framework of their cosmology. To accept the evidence of their own senses and the assurance of their own hearts, they would have to rethink their scheme of things.

On the other hand, some are immediately convinced;

the conversation they have had with the one they loved has been too filled with mutual memories and personal evidential to leave any room for doubt. They are likely to greet me, when I waken, with tears of joy. I know how they feel. All that has just happened to them has also happened to me.

Many are profoundly grateful to me personally. They forget that in trance I am only an instrument. I have no idea what they have heard or experienced. I care, just as a priest or minister or doctor cares, and yet if I am to be a good medium I have to keep myself out of their problems— just as a good minister or doctor has to remain uninvolved. A psychiatrist also knows the warmth with which a patient identifies with the one who does him a great psychological service. Sometimes a young man or young woman identifies me with the discarnate father with whom he has been talking. The young person comes back again and again and then begins to call me on the telephone wanting advice, just as if I had been in on all that transpired in the trance.

More disconcerting, not infrequently a widow begins to identify me with her deceased husband! When I sense that such gratitude is becoming personal I have to be busy when she wants another sitting; I can't have her weeping on my shoulder no matter how badly she needs a shoulder. A conscientious medium has his problems.

At the same time some clients have become my treasured friends. Dr. Sherwood Eddy is an outstanding example. It was in 1938 that he first came to me in London. He felt that messages from his father and mother and from certain friends could have come from no other sources than the ones Fletcher named, and he continued to collect evidence through other mediums in other parts of the world. Then in November, 1940, he arrived at my door again, this time in California. With him was a friend he had met only a quarter hour previous—Gerald Heard, formerly science commentator on the British Broadcasting Company and a writer of many interests. Mr. Heard was then new in California and at that time I had read none of his books, nor Mr. Eddy's, although I knew Eddy's work as World Secretary of the Young Men's Christian Association very well.

Later Eddy published some of his notes on that day's sitting. Mr. Heard seems to have been impressed by Fletcher's comments on the various members of his family, but it was the advent of the Irish poet, George Russell, and of the sociologist, Havelock Ellis, which most interested them. Unknown to each other, both men had known Russell and Ellis. Russell said to Heard, "I have a better beard than you have." He then asked for a pencil and Fletcher—or I in my sleep, as you will—signed the initials Æ in characteristic manner. Said Russell, "I have tried to keep all the windows of my life open on all sides. We have things and places here but nothing enchains us."

It was in that sitting that a Chinese admiral reminded Eddy that Eddy had stood beside the admiral's casket when he was killed; then the admiral commented on Chiang Kai-shek, "He still reads your Bible but he is a kind of Old Testament Christian." Eddy had given Chiang his marked Bible.

Havelock Ellis came on the scene to comment that he had known both Heard and Eddy but that neither of them knew that he knew the other. Eddy asked Ellis what he and Ellis had talked about the day of Eddy's call at the Ellis home and Ellis responded with considerable detail, adding, "I am still occupied here with the subject of sex and war."

Dr. Eddy's sittings are often the equivalent of a world seminar with the space-time barriers down. In one sitting, for which a mutual friend showed me the notes, Bishop Azariah, the grand old man of the Indian Anglican Church, appeared, discussing the present state of Christianity in India, and reminding Eddy of their pact to pray together at the same time every day, a pact which Eddy had kept with him for more than forty years . . . Then a doctor who had run a leper hospital on Formosa . . . Then an Indian YMCA secretary who had first met Eddy in Mysore, saying that hundreds of students used to consider Eddy next to Jesus the most important personality in bringing the Kingdom of Heaven to pass on earth . . . Then an archbishop of the Russian church, reminding Eddy that they had first met in Poland, and assuring him that behind the Iron Curtain the fires of religious faith now burn more brightly and are tended more faithfully than ever . . . Then Baron Paul Von Schreinach, who identified himself as the general in command of the Fifteenth Hussars in World War I; later he had organized and led a German pacifist movement and reminded Eddy that he had met him during the Third Reich the summer before their friend was shot in Berlin . . . Then a man who gave his name as Campbell and said he had died just a few hours previously; he remarked that the shadow of Canterbury was becoming increasingly dark and discussed its past history, as well as the background of London City Temple, in terms of the men they had both known. Said Campbell, "It is literally true that you are encompassed by a great cloud of witnesses. The future of the Protestant faith is in the hands of people who can blend mysticism with the social gospel which together make up the whole program of Christianity. This problem has to be met *now* on earth. It's easy to see it after you get over here. In immediate terms there is the problem of stemming the anti-Western tide in Asia in face of the white-dominated racial discrimination in

South Africa and the southern United States. The color problem can lick the West in the end unless it is solved with equality and justice." . . . Someone named Joshi brought his greetings and said he got his start at the YMCA in Bombay where he caught from Eddy the urge to organize the Untouchables in a labor movement. He worked with Nathan Salananda, he said. "The last time you visited with Gandhidje I was there. In fact I was within hearing distance when Gandhi was shot. Gandhi is still influencing people. You see, he radiates his influence in the same way that Christ and Buddha and Ramakrishna and all the great teachers radiate their personality; I can't explain it, but it is a matter of degree." . . . A former editor of the *Bombay Times* brought greetings and said if he could get across only one message it would be that very few individuals are sufficiently dedicated to have enough influence to effect a change in the world. "God is the goal, Jesus Christ is the Way. Buddha, Gandhi, everyone can be a Way, or a Way-shower to the degree of their being. You see, God still speaks through people. In this new age the veil is becoming very thin between the seen and unseen aspects of the universe. The artificial barriers of race, creed and national boundaries will be no more; they are already gone, in essence, if people could but see. The United Nations is pointing in the right direction. These developments take time. Remember that it took three hundred years before the Christian church made a noticeable impact, and a hundred years before the Constitution of the United States was accepted. In faith, give the United Nations time." . . . A doctor, formerly located in Turkey, apprised Eddy of his death a few weeks previously. "I just checked out of Beirut and into heaven. I'm never far from you when you are about your Father's business. Go on to Russia this summer without fear. Your trip will again bear more fruit than you dream." . . . Then a Dr. Mark Ward, once a missionary in the Near East and since his death often an adviser to Eddy when Eddy was traveling in that part of the world, discussed the old Armenian conflict and its relationship to present disturbances in the Near East . . . Ruth Finley, who identified herself as the Joan of the Stewart Edward White books, made some comments to a friend who was sitting with Dr. Eddy, and then said to Eddy, "I heard you at Oberlin years ago. You were introduced by Dr. Leacock and you almost persuaded me to become a Student Volunteer but I broke the spell by going to work for the *Cleveland News* and *Plain Dealer*." . . . Andrew D. Harmon, a former university president and once a member of an Eddy seminar, commented, "The secret of the tremendous influence of certain religious groups is the fact they are not centered in a priesthood. Among them every Christian is a witness, as in the early church. To be sure, there has to be some professional service in the line of finance and practicalities, but the important matter is the bearing of individual witness. Shall it be a small witness or a large witness? Why limit God or budget the universe? You can pray for wisdom to make your whole life effective or you can pray about some problem of the moment. Think big for God is big. Be audacious, very audacious. When you address groups, always say something about the spiritual world of power which people can use." . . . Several members of Eddy's family also came with personal and sometimes highly practical comments and suggestions.

And so ended another Sherwood Eddy Seminar! When I saw the notes, of which these are sketchy abstractions, I pondered anew the reach of one man who gives his life to his fellows on a world-wide scale—and expects eternity to co-operate.

Through Dr. Eddy another interesting friend came into my life, although I certainly did not guess at the time that she would become a friend nor that Eddy had sent her. The place was also California and the time the early forties. I had just finished packing to take off on vacation and had no intention of seeing anyone, but unfortunately when the doorbell rang I answered it myself. An elderly woman, very plainly dressed and tight-lipped, asked for a sitting. I explained that I was leaving and tried politely to close the door. But the woman practically kept her foot in the door; she had come to see me and she intended to see me. After some argument I decided that she belonged to the screwball company who go from medium to medium and never give up, and that the quickest way to be rid of her was to accede to her demands.

After the sitting, my taciturn client made no comment as to what she had received from her discarnate friends. But when I returned from my trip she came again. And then she gave me her name—Mrs. Emmons Blaine, of Chicago. I was all but stunned, for I knew some of the friends of the McCormick family and their position of leadership in many civic enterprises. Finally she told me that it was her great friend Sherwood Eddy who had sent her, and that she had come against her own inclination.

After she and I became friends, Dr. Eddy told me that she had been the means of an outstanding answer to prayer in a time of his need. "It is in such instances that the psychic and the spiritual meet," he commented. At the time when he was first pressed to take on the world secretaryship of the YMCA he was held back by the knowledge that he could not carry his prior responsibility for India, maintain his voluminous correspondence and do the required amount of traveling without a full-time secretary. And a secretary to travel with him was an item he felt the YMCA Board could not afford. So he prayed that God would meet his need. He told me that he said to God very succinctly, "Now this is your business, Father. It looks to me as if I need a secretary but if You have a better idea, that is entirely up to You. I am not going to keep on asking You. I'm just putting myself in Your hands and asking You this once." A few days later he reached Chicago where he was to make a speech. Mrs. Blaine took him to her beautiful home for lunch and afterward drove him to his next appointment. On the way she said to him, "I've been turning over in my mind this far-reaching new responsibility you are taking on, and it occurs to me that you should have the service of a full-time secretary to travel with you; some young man to take off your shoulders as much of the routine work as possible. And I should like to take care of the expense of this secretary." Quite simply, Eddy accepted. In his eyes she was God's fellow worker.

And I might add that since her death he has seldom had a sitting at which she has not appeared with words of counsel. Her interest in the investment of her fortune in the causes designated in her will seems not to have abated. Obviously, I see only the transcription of the notes, but Eddy, as well as others who have shared sittings with him, pass on such a wealth of what might be called character evidence, or personality expression, that I feel this unusual woman to have met the tests of identification.

It never does to judge a lady by her clothes, at least not when she has come for a sitting. She may be attempting a kind of disguise, or grief may have given her a sartorial indifference foreign to her real nature. I recall a weird little Englishwoman who came to me in London. If I ever saw a forlorn creature it was this lonely, helpless-looking individual. She had her sitting and I wakened to find her appraising me with sharp eyes; I thought she was wondering

how much I was likely to charge her. Having just finished
a series of free sittings for persons who could not afford to
pay but whose needs were known to Maurice Barbanell
and the staff of *The Psychic News*, I had already determined at her entrance that she might as well be the thirty-
first. So I told her there was no charge. The way that poor
creature bristled! She was not merely insulted; she was
mad. "Young man, if you think I don't have money because I look like hell, you're mistaken," and she handed me
twenty pounds—then about one hundred dollars. Two
weeks later she came again for another sitting. This time
she was smartly dressed, her hair was done, she carried herself with an air. I asked no questions but when the sitting
was over she told me that on the first occasion her sister
had come, the sister whose death had plunged her into
grief and despair. The sister had identified herself past all
doubt and had told her to get herself together, to hire a
chauffeur for their car, and to go to living. And this she
had already done!

Sometimes a client who comes to me initiates a chain
of events. For instance, two editors of a well-known publishing house found that following publication by another
house of a popular book on reincarnation, they were receiving an unusual number of manuscripts dealing with
psychic matters. One of them, a vice-president whom we
shall call Smith, suggested to a woman assistant, whom we
shall call Jones, that they call on me, more to satisfy their
curiosity than with the expectation of receiving enlighten-
ment. Smith made the appointment, without mentioning
his profession or his reason for coming. By the night of
the sitting Smith and Jones had collected three other
friends so that it was a group of five which I admitted to
my New York apartment. They seated themselves comfortably; we exchanged brief remarks; I leaned back in

my big red leather chair, put a black mask over my eyes to keep out the light, and promptly went to sleep.

In the course of the trance two former editors of the firm to which Smith and Jones belonged discussed publishing plans and sent personal messages to their families. Then came Professor James H. Hyslop, formerly professor of logic and ethics at Columbia University and, until his death in 1920, one of the distinguished officers of the American Society for Psychical Research.

Professor Hyslop inquired, chattily, why they did not do more publishing in the psychic field and mentioned one of their recent publications, a rather scholarly approach to parapsychological interests which had been especially well received. The editors acknowledged their pride in that book. Whereupon Professor Hyslop averred, "You will be proud of my book, too."

Having no idea who Professor Hyslop might be, or had been, Smith replied, "But we don't have a book by you, Professor Hyslop."

"My manuscript ought to be on your desk," said Hyslop, genially. "I say 'my' but actually it is the record of some of my work with Miss Tubby since my death."

"The manuscript wasn't there when I left the office," Smith protested.

"If it isn't there now, you'll have it in the next two or three days," said the redoubtable Hyslop, "and you'll see its significance fast enough." Then he appended a bit of Hyslopian advice, "You ought to do more of this sort of publishing and not so much sweetness and light."

Two evenings later Smith arrived at a dinner meeting with a six-hundred-page tome under his arm. Approaching Jones, he proffered the manuscript. "This is Hyslop!"

Jones took the manuscript home but had read only a few chapters when a fortnight later she accompanied another curious colleague to my apartment. One of the first arrivals among the unseen conversants was Professor Hyslop. Said Hyslop to Jones, "I see my manuscript is now on your desk. And I know exactly what you'll say about it. You'll say it's too wordy as it stands. It's actually too exact; too much verbatim recording. But you'll also say that it has very significant material—and you'll be right on both scores."

Some six weeks later Jones returned for another sitting and Professor Hyslop was waiting at the threshold.

"I almost did not come," said Jones, "because I have not yet finished your manuscript. A press of work."

"I know, I know," Hyslop replied. "It's hard to read anything with so many handwritten insertions. But it doesn't matter whether you've finished it. In a couple of days you'll be meeting Tubby and you two can take up from there."

Jones knew from the return address on the manuscript that Miss Tubby lived in Montclair, New Jersey, but she had no idea of going to Montclair. However, two days later she unexpectedly drove through the city, telephoned to Miss Tubby, and of course went to see her. Being this near, she said to herself, who can resist foreordination? Thinking to bowl over Miss Tubby, she reported the whole incident. Tubby was not bowled over. "That's Professor Hyslop," she agreed. "He never gives up."

Dr. Marcus Bach of the University of Iowa is another who started a chain of events and a stream of persons, important because some of the people have been in deep personal need of evidence that life goes on. When Bach himself first participated in a trance sitting for which I was the medium, he was not expecting much in the way of personal evidence. His travels have taken him to many of the less well known sections of the world to interview men and women who are the leaders of one or another cause or cult. Many of these persons have supernormal powers. Besides, he had sat with sensitives in India, Guatemala, Haiti, Africa and other corners of the world and had a trained ear for psychic matters. But he was not in a mood of expectation that night in Iowa City.

This first meeting was arranged by a mutual friend, Dr. Lewis Dunnington, but took place in the Bach home. There were about twenty persons present and a tape recorder reported all that transpired. At one point Fletcher commented to Bach that he should contact Leonard Deaver. "He is a good boy and you should have him with you in your work." Bach asked who Leonard Deaver might be. "A minister," Fletcher told him. "Salem Church."

Neither the name nor the church registered with Bach, so he asked for more information and Fletcher reported that Deaver was pastor of a church in a nearby town. Bach then asked from whom this message was coming and Fletcher gave the name, "Russell Walker." However, Bach had never heard of Russell Walker either, so he asked who Walker was, when he had died and how he knew Leonard Deaver.

Said Fletcher, "Russell Walker was a train conductor. Leonard Deaver was in charge of his funeral. He buried him."

After the session Bach consulted his yearbook of ministers and other lists but could not locate a Leonard Deaver. However, about a week later when he picked up his day's mail he noticed on one envelope the return address, "Salem Church." Laughing to himself, he tore open the envelope and found the letter signed Leonard Deaver. Pastor Deaver was inviting Bach to his church to lecture on his travels.

Bach called the Rev. Mr. Deaver and before he concluded the conversation he asked if Mr. Deaver had ever heard of Arthur Ford; he had not. Had he ever heard of Russell Walker? He had conducted his funeral a few weeks previous. So Bach asked Walker's business. "A train conductor."

The result of our first session has been other group meetings in Iowa City, but to detail their ramifications would require quite a spread. For me, one man made all the meetings worthwhile—a professional man who had never been able to believe in life after death, but who was so impressed by what he heard in the seance that he called his son at midnight to come hear the recording of the session. His own joy, his relief, his sudden shifting of perspective and hence of values was a transforming experience.

And so it goes.

CHAPTER 11

Colleagues Across the Border

NOT INFREQUENTLY professional people ask for a sitting in order to get advice from discarnate colleagues. I may or may not know their purpose at the time. One really famous name in the field of research in extrasensory perception came to me for five successive days at the same hour, incognito, accompanied by Miss Tubby. Not only did she never introduce the man but when we met on other occasions she never even referred to him. For several years he returned for his annual series of sittings. Then one day I met him socially and learned his name, whereupon he came no more. Later I found that some of his published work was based upon those sittings but he did not quote Fletcher, nor do I quote him.

In the matter of specialists consulting their colleagues not only is it true that the best stories cannot be told, but the fact that I often do not hear the result of a seance until years after it took place leads me to surmise that some of the most evidential sittings remain unknown to me. I have sat for many persons in government circles—congressmen, senators, members of the State Department and special agencies; for generals and admirals, ambassadors, special envoys and others in extremely high places. During World War II seances were often set under conditions of great

114

caution and sometimes the sitters were not introduced to me although I frequently recognized them. Since the time of these planned meetings many of the individuals have continued to come to me once or twice a year.

Usually an individual seeking professional help merely waits for Fletcher to say that the one he came to consult is present, or to name some other who has a professional interest in him. But occasionally the sitter may ask for a special friend and Fletcher may respond, "I think he is here but he hasn't come into focus yet," or "Your friend isn't here now but maybe I can reach him." Fletcher once commented, "We have our equivalent of the telephone." Whatever the means on the unseen plane of sending out the call, it frequently happens that the desired person shows up before my trance is over. Fletcher will say, "Your friend is here now." Or sometimes he will say, "We can't get the help you need at this time, but we think we can get it to you in the next few days." And within the next few days a series of "coincidences" will produce the solution.

Sometimes scientists get together in my trance! At a sitting attended by a group which included a young anthropologist who had received her B. A. degree from Drake University and her brother who was about to receive his doctorate from the University of Chicago, an invisible scientist gave his name as Forest Moulton. He began with personal comments and then said to the anthropologist, "I once received an honorary degree from the school which gave you your bachelor of arts." Then to the brother he said, "And I won my doctorate from the same university which is about to bestow yours." Later when *Who's Who* was consulted it was found that Professor Moulton had indeed received an honorary LL.D from Drake in 1939 and had earned his Ph.D degree from the University of Chicago in 1899.

The point of Moulton's appearance, however, was a message he wanted to send to an uncle of the young people for whom he seemed to have high regard. "Tell your uncle that I used to wish I could take a ride on an asteroid. Well, now you might say I've ridden on an asteroid! But don't give him the idea that I do nothing but ride on asteroids. I'm working just as diligently as I ever worked, and I now know more about space than I ever dreamed there was to know. Tell your uncle that the more I sense the laws of the universe the greater my awe for That Which lies behind the laws. And tell him that now I know that the Power which holds the universe in relationship is as much compassion as law. Without either, in this immeasurable immensity of time-space, the worlds would fall apart. I wish I'd known both halves of the equation before I came here—the love with the law. Tell him that."

One day a Japanese came with his interpreter, explaining that he was a member of the engineering faculty of the University of Tokyo and that he had some questions to ask of me in trance. He asked permission to use his camera. What his questions were I do not know but at one point Fletcher had difficulty in getting a point through from an unseen Japanese colleague, whereupon Fletcher said, "He is writing it out; give me a pencil and I'll draw you what I see." A pencil was handed to me whereupon I sat up, they tell me, and began to draw. The result was the Japanese characters sufficiently clear so that the two Japanese could read the message. They sent me a photograph of myself asleep but reproducing the message Fletcher was seeing.

Another scientist attending a seance received a bit of information which interested him because the element of precognition was in play. Dr. William F. G. Swann, director of Bartol Research Foundation, formerly director of Sloane Laboratory, Yale University, came to dinner one night in November, 1955, at the home of Melvin L. Sutley, superintendent of Wills Eye Hospital, Philadelphia. I was Sutley's house guest and, as I recall, the men who came after dinner were not introduced to me. Even so, after the seance, during which one of the doctors felt he had been overwhelmed by the mass of personal detail of his life that Fletcher had given him, this doctor accused me of having read *Who's Who*. "Are you in *Who's Who?*" I asked rather automatically. "No, but my grandfather is." Amazing the people who expect me to carry *Who's Who*, both British and American and in several editions, up my sleeve for instant reference.

Back to Swann. During the trance, Dr. Swann's first wife, Mabel, spoke of acquaintances and incidents in her life which Swann later had to verify in order to authenticate them. Then Mabel said that Swann's old college in England planned to invite him to participate in some distinguished occasion. Fletcher commented that "there is a man here named H—— who tells her that as rector of the college he is very proud of Swann. His name is Sir R—— H——. Mabel advises Swann to accept the invitation and says, 'You may come back with some more letters after your name.'" Swann could not recall the name of Sir R—— H——, as there was no rector of the college in his day. However, he consulted the British *Who's Who* and found that Sir R—— M—— H—— had been rector of the college since 1948. No mention was made of his resignation or death. Dr. Swann dropped the matter from his mind. The following March, five months after the seance, he received a letter from his college, informing him that the governors had elected him to honorary fellowship of the college, and that he was invited to attend the annual celebration of commemoration day the following autumn and receive the award. The letter was signed R—— P—— L——, Rector. Swann accepted. However, he was confused by the

fact that the rector was R—— P—— L—— instead of Sir
R—— M—— H—— as cited in *Who's Who*. The only solution was that Sir R—— M—— H—— must have resigned
or died. Swann consulted the obituaries in a scientific
journal and found that Sir R—— M—— H—— had died
before the date of the seance. Swann subsequently attended
the ceremonies and received the award.

One day at a seance in Chicago a discarnate who gave
his name as Ralph Yerkes discussed the relationship of the
wild cells found in cancer to the problem of mental direction,
conscious and unconscious, of cell development. His final
comment was:

Of course we don't know what energy is. We use the term
electromagnetic currents but we don't know what we mean by
that either. From here I can see that the stream of life, enduring
consciousness, finds expression wherever the physical instrument
is capable of manipulation or growth. It is possible to choose how
much life energy to use—and how and where—just as you have
a right to determine how much water to use from the lake in
front of you. You can close the faucet or let in a trickle or allow
it to come full blast. The decision depends upon the goal, the
thinking, purpose, determination.

One of the sitters at that seance remarked that sometimes
it seemed as if, during meditation, the incoming energy
were too much, as if it would almost blow an individual
apart. Whereupon another discarnate picked up Yerkes'
figure of the faucet:

Sometimes the water main bursts but that is not the fault of
the lake. It depends upon the structure of the main. . . .The current of energy, which we don't understand, responds to demand
and need. Moreover, the demand is usually determined by our
need. For instance, a person in extreme danger feels the need for
self-preservation and forces a demand for strength he never

deemed possible before. Strength and energy come when a person abandons himself completely, when he draws his ego completely into the stream, knowing he has no other escape. He generally receives help because he has eliminated the mental and spiritual blocks in the way. In a sense fear is very much akin to faith in that it drives a person to complete abandon. He knows he has no lower depth to suffer; therefore, what can he lose. He has accepted the fact that humanly he has gone the limit. There is nothing more to fear so he is willing to try. Then comes his healing. The ancients said, 'The fear of God is the beginning of wisdom.' They did not mean fright but a sense of awe, amazement, grandeur, a knowledge that something beyond the self can comprehend the self's need.

I am concerned to bring these matters to the attention of people. It is very frustrating here, after a liftetime of battling for causes, to see so few willing to be used to carry on. Often people on earth lament our loss when all the time we could have this continuing kinship. We are all together, you and us, but the black curtain of ignorance drops between us. Rip the curtain apart!

A biologist, Carroll B. Nash, who is director of the Parapsychology Laboratory of St. Joseph's College in Philadelphia, has been part of a group with whom I periodically hold sittings. He is attempting, among other objectives, to determine what factors affect an individual's expression of psi; in other words what makes a person a better sensitive at certain times. As a medium I am interested in co-operating in Dr. Nash's experiments because I would like to find out what makes my own work more effective under certain conditions.

Artists come to receive help from discarnate colleagues. I recall Bessie Clark Drouet especially because she worked directly with her materials under an invisible instructor who coached her while I was in trance. When I first knew her she was a painter, and a very successful one. In a seance Fletcher once told her that a sculptor on his plane wanted to tell her that she would also make a fine sculptor. Shortly after that she tried her first work with clay, and at her next sitting a discarnate sculptor of such note commented on her technique that she would not believe he could be the personality he purported to be. Indeed, Mrs. Drouet long hesitated to mention his name lest she be deluding herself or perhaps belittling the noted sculptor. In the following years she did some fine work and from the reported conversations with this teacher I would say it was not improbable that so great a man might be interested in helping a fellow artist in this unusual fashion. Over a period of several weeks she did a bust of me and whenever certain details gave her difficulty, I would simply lean back and slip into trance while she got the needed suggestions.

Buell Mullen, muralist, has frequently come to discuss her assignments with former colleagues. She is particularly known for her paintings on stainless steel, a form of art which presents its own problems. Her murals are found in the new General Electric Building in Detroit; in Case Institute in Cleveland; in the United States Naval Academy at Annapolis; the Library of Congress; the Brazilian Ministry of Public Works; and many other places. Recently she wrote to me:

Several times in trance, both in class and in private sittings, you have said that a famous architect who died about eight years ago, Paul Cret, was there. I have asked him definite questions about solutions to some artistic problem, such as which theme to develop, and he has discussed the problem clearly. One time he suggested a theme which was completely new to me, and while in the end I did not use the form he suggested, he opened up an excellent new concept which proved most successful.

On one occasion, while I was working on a very large mural project, I found unreasonable and, to me, unaccountable opposition on the part of the architect. Your trance was of great assistance, for Paul Cret told me of the real reason and problem behind the antagonism and with his help I was able to work it all out harmoniously.

Many times you—or those speaking through you—have clarified delays in my work, or made plain some hidden personal reluctance towards a project, and several times you have given me word of commissions which were shaping, of which I knew nothing, but which have later come into being. . . .

And I think the instance of the strong visual impression of Tom Kelly of Pendle Hill that led to sketching his portrait, from the experience in class, was artistically most fascinating. I do feel, most strongly, that the inspirational side of my work, the creation of the symbolic themes, has been accelerated and sometimes directly inspired by the guidance coming through your trance.

Lawyers come to Fletcher. Recently a woman lawyer came with a baffling inheritance case, and after the session she told me that she had got in touch with the former dean of her law school and received just the help she needed. Financial experts come for aid in planning investments, and I do not mean stock market manipulations. One such expert is adviser for a chain of banks on wills in which persons want to leave sums for eleemosynary purposes. Some far-reaching ideas have come through these seances, ideas which have fired projects that will affect medical history.

Editors have come to talk with former colleagues about the hiring of new personnel. Authors have come with problems regarding characters in their books, but on one occasion it was the character who came with a problem about the author. In this case the character was a discarnate!

One day a man called the editor of a publishing company, gave his name and said that his mother-in-law, an acquaintance of the editor's, had recently died and had left a request that some member of the family try to get in touch with her through a medium, and she had mentioned this editor as one who knew a medium. So the editor gave the man my name. The next day the man called again to say he had reached his mother-in-law and to ask if the name Frank (a borrowed name) would mean anything. Yes, it would, said the editor; it was the name of one of a group of pioneers about whom he was presently publishing a book.

"It means nothing to me," said the man on the telephone, "but this chap Frank showed up at the seance and says he wants very much to talk with you as soon as convenient."

Without explanation, the editor came to me for a sitting. And Frank came to the editor and gave the full account of his own death, along with his friends. Names, places, incidents of former years were given, suggestions made as to measures which their wives should follow, and pertinent observations made on the book.

Through the years a good many persons have come with medical problems. What they get in the way of help depends, of course, upon who among their discarnate friends comes to talk with them. Although I know as little as a modestly educated adult could know about physiology and much less than that about medicine, I am particularly interested in these consultations.

In my early days of working for the British College of Psychical Science, I once wakened from trance to find a woman client filled with ire, accusing me of being a fraud, insisting that I had fabricated a ridiculous story. Fletcher had said that her husband had cancer of the tongue and that if it was not taken care of immediately the consequences would be sad. She wanted me to know that her husband was a big, strong man, without an ailment of any kind, and moreover he never kept anything from her. Whereupon she went to the registrar and demanded, and got, her money back.

Two days later came a letter. She had gone home and reported the duplicity of the American medium to her husband, who had then admitted that he did have a lump on his tongue and that it was growing, but that he had kept telling himself it would soon go away and so had said nothing about it. The day following the seance he went to a doctor, was sent at once to a hospital for an operation, and the wife was now enclosing a check. Would they thank the young American medium for a most helpful disclosure?

Some clients regularly ask for medical aid. In fact, they have regular medical advisers on the other side, discarnates who discuss their present state of health, comment on current treatment and make suggestions. Occasionally a client brings his earth-side physician to the sitting. I recall a family of five who came to me in Chicago in 1955—a mother, one son who was a college professor, his wife, and a daughter and her husband both of whom were medical physicians. After I was in trance the mother asked Fletcher if there were a physician at hand, and upon being assured that a Dr. Tucker was ready to help them, she requested that he look over the group to see if anyone of those present needed medical aid. No mention was made of the fact that only three days previous the daughter-in-law had come out of a month's stay in a hospital. Dr. Tucker promptly designated the patient, discussed past and present treatment with the two doctors present, made suggestions, and then asked the young woman why she had said so little about her headaches. He told her the cause, suggested that an osteopathic physician could readily remedy it, and then made comments to the doctors on the use of osteopathy to medicine, as seen from his perspective.

The mother then said to Dr. Tucker, "Would you please take a look at my daughter's baby?" The child was some forty miles distant in an unnamed suburb. No mention was made of the fact that a few days earlier when the baby had her three-month checkup, it had been noted that one hip appeared rotated and the parents had some concern. Dr. Tucker said, "Oh, she's so young there isn't much to her yet." The grandmother persisted, "Still, I'd be glad if you'd look." Half a minute later **Dr. Tucker** commented, through the sleeping medium of course, "I see what you mean—that left hip." He then explained that it looked to him as if it would right itself, but that if it did not the baby's father could take her to Boston in a year or two and have some corrective work done.

It was after that sitting that the baby's father is reported to have said, in the tone of one who would brush off a marvel with a whisk of scientific authority, "A very good demonstration of mental telepathy."

Said his wife, "But, dear, when we went in there we didn't believe in telepathy."

It was that same woman doctor who remarked, some months later, after more experience, "According to the law of parsimony the simplest explanation with the fewest loose ends is Fletcher's contention that discarnate minds still operate."

Sometimes the medical advice of discarnate doctors contains diagnostic elements which living doctors have not noted, and sometimes the living doctors have the edge, for not all discarnate physicians keep up with the latest in modern medicine! Sherwood Eddy is the kind of patient who quotes the visible and invisible doctors to one another. When both sets of doctors decree rest at a time when he feels he must start off on a seminar to Asia or Europe, he shakes his eighty-seven-year-old head and explains that he has to carry out his present assignment and will they please —visible and invisible—do what they can for him.

Recently a friend brought Mrs. Harold Ruopp of Minneapolis to see me. At the time I knew nothing about Mrs. Ruopp and her work with American children and their foreign pen-pals in behalf of peace, nor about her husband, Harold Ruopp, who was formerly pastor of the Hennepin Avenue Methodist Church, Minneapolis, and so naturally I did not know that Mr. Ruopp had had a long illness belatedly diagnosed as sprue. As soon as I was in trance a friend of the Ruopps came in with Fletcher and introduced a Dr. Cochrane, once on the staff of an American hospital in China, and much interested in sprue. Dr. Cochrane discussed the case as seen by his colleagues and himself from their present point of view. He went into the matter of multiple allergies and lack of protein absorption, discussed work done on sprue which apparently had not come to the attention of the physicians attending Mr. Ruopp, commented in detail upon diet and the use of larger doses of certain vitamins, pointed out the advantages to the patient of a move to Arizona where he could sit out in the sun and absorb its actinic rays, and finally specified some further tests which might be made.

Two days later, when Mrs. Ruopp returned home, she found that a German physician, recently engaged in allergy research in another part of the country, had come onto the staff of the hospital in which her husband was a patient. The German physician made a bone marrow test which corroborated the findings of the seance, of which he knew nothing, and he planned a regime in line with Dr. Cochrane's suggestions. The seance was probably most useful in giving the patient confidence in a changed regime where previously he had felt that further efforts were of no avail. Moreover, close and valued friends of his, now discarnate, had also spoken to his wife, sending messages of confidence in his ultimate recovery and restored usefulness. The impression of the hour's consultation was of a group of interested medical men pooling their insight in general consultation, and of warm friends expressing practical ideas about financial problems, planning the trip West, offering suggestions about the best person to assist in finding lodging and other practical matters. Again discarnate friends had proved the practicality of their continuing interest.

I recall an occasion when a young Chinese couple came

for medical aid because the beautiful young wife had not been able to become pregnant. Their unseen medical adviser was a Chinese physician who had been acquainted with the young woman's father at the University of Nanking. He made an interesting diagnosis of the husband as well as of the wife with suggestions as to enriched diet and a changed mode of living.

There are several psychiatrists who both send and bring patients for sittings. Two medical psychiatrists are currently working on cases of possession. While sometimes schizophrenia masks as possession, at other times the suspicion of possession proves to be well founded. The discarnate physician is able to explain first why this patient is open to possession; that is, what the emotional trait is that has affected the endocrine and nervous systems in such fashion that consciousness can be partially displaced by a discarnate entity seeking a body for temporary aggrandizement. He then explains the plight of the possessing entity— why he feels earth-bound, what he is trying to accomplish. Finally, therapy is suggested both for the patient and for the discarnate who is more easily reached by an earth mind than by another discarnate. The entity can usually be persuaded to go about the business of his own development. It is then possible to deal more readily with the patient.

For many years Dr. Russell G. MacRobert of New York has utilized my trance clairvoyance for diagnostic purposes. It was Robert Norwood, when he was minister of St. Bartholomew's, who brought us together. Typical of MacRobert's work with Fletcher is this case lifted from his notebook:

I accompanied a senior college student, a patient undergoing analysis, at his request, on his first visit to Ford. He had heard Ford give a public lecture but had had no personal communication with him. During Ford's trance I sat to one side and made my own rapid notes. Among twenty names mentioned nine were difficult foreign names, all except one were known to the patient; six bore on the discussion of the patient's life and problems; five names I myself recognized as belonging to deceased psychiatrists and former associates who made interspersed personal remarks to me.

A serious story wound around that one unidentified name. Fletcher, prompted by his invisible communicators, said that when the patient was a child of three a young uncle of sixteen, whose name he gave in both the foreign and American versions, had hanged himself in the bathroom of the home of the child's parents. This tragic incident had been a well-guarded family secret. Until informed by Fletcher, the patient had never heard of such an uncle. Fletcher gave many descriptive details of the habits and character of the uncle. He intimated some psychic traumatism to the patient at the time, but what he described as important was the continuing influence of the dead uncle's presence on the patient up to the time of this interview. The father of the patient later verified the story. Using the psychically imparted information, Dr. MacRobert was able to deal successfully with the disturbed patient.

Judging from my own clientele an increasing number of psychiatrists are interested in parapsychology. Dr. MacRobert has collected a few supportive statistics. In 1948 he attempted to survey the current interest of his colleagues in extrasensory perception. He made his survey in the form of a five-item questionnaire which was sent to all those listed in the 1947 membership roll of the Association for Research in Nervous and Mental Disease and in the directory of the American Board of Psychiatry and Neurology. Between mid-April and the end of August, 1948, the questionnaire was assumed to have reached 2,510 specialists of whom 28.8 per cent, or 723, responded—a high return by the standards of professional pollsters. Among those who answered were most of the names of the active and eminent members of the two groups.

Question 3 asked: Do you believe that psychiatrists and neurologists would serve a useful purpose by sponsoring research to determine if extrasensory perception has a place in the psychodynamics of the nervous system? In reply, 495 (68 per cent) answered *yes;* 129 (18 per cent) *no;* and 99 (14 per cent) were undecided.

Question 4 asked: Have you ever observed, in your general or professional experience or professional practice, anything which would indicate an extrasensory awareness? The answer from 163 respondents (23 per cent) was *yes;* from 437 (60 per cent) *no;* and 123 (17 per cent) were uncertain. With their answers many of the specialists sent personal letters containing pertinent comment.

Personally I feel that so much is to be gained through the co-operation of psychiatrists and mediums, when both are skilled in discrimination, that I try to make time against almost any odds to co-operate.

CHAPTER 12

Down Under

IN THE DOZEN YEARS between 1928 and World War II, I did considerable traveling, sometimes because of lecture appointments, sometimes because a series of private sittings had been arranged, and sometimes because my own curiosity led me forth. In 1928 I first visited Germany for a combination of these reasons.

My good friend Florizel Reuter wanted me to give some sittings for friends of his. He and his mother had been my house guests in London and I was now, for several weeks, fellow guests with them in the enormous fifteenth-century castle of the Princess Victoria Reuss. I spent several weeks at the castle. The Princess was really a plump German hausfrau with a heart of gold, as the villagers always pointed out. The palace was overrun with rats which dashed boldly into the elaborate corridors and hid under draperies. At night the hausfrau would dominate; she would give orders to have the rats caught in the big wire cages kept handy for that purpose, but in the morning the kind heart would win out and she would have them turned loose again.

A second reason for my trip to Germany was my promise to give several evenings to the Berlin Society for Psychical Research. At that time there was considerable interest in psychic matters in Germany. Indeed, from the early days of Mesmer on, interest had never abated and German physicians who were using hypnotism as a means of a patient's making a self-diagnosis were bound at times to uncover other psychic states. Hence a few reliable German mediums had developed. There was a healthy climate for experimentation; a constrained eagerness checked by the good German insistence upon documentation. Baron Schrenck-Notzing was carrying on important laboratory experiments in Munich. He was a physician and psychiatrist who had come to his interest in psychic phenomena by way of hypnotic work with disturbed patients, and his findings were heeded by other European and British medical men.

In Berlin I recall that there were six reporters from leading German newspapers present in a large audience. One of the reporters later showed me the notes he had taken on the clairvoyant messages and the audience response, commenting: "If I were to hand in for publication what I have just written I would lose my place on the paper." Before I left Berlin some of the pressmen got together on a final statement to the effect that although Ford knew no German, still they had found that 70 per cent of his descriptions of departed friends were immediately recognized by surprised members of the audience; 20 per cent had been carefully traced and verified; and 10 per cent remained unidentified. Baron Schrenck-Notzing was delighted with the report.

It was Schrenck-Notzing's work with two of his proteges which furnished my third reason for going to Germany. I wanted to see the mediumship of the two Austrian mediums, Willi and Rudi Schneider. Willi's control, known as Olga, purported to be the former mistress of Ludwig I, the old King of Bavaria. During a seance one night when

Willi was about seventeen, Olga insisted that the power was not strong enough and that Rudi must assist. The father, a linotype operator with practical common sense, responded that Rudi was too young and besides he was in bed asleep. A few moments later the door opened and Rudi entered, in deep trance. From then on Olga controlled Rudi.

Everyone interested in psychic matters in Britain, on the Continent, and in America knew about the physical mediumship of these two young chaps, for few mediums have been more thoroughly studied by a wider variety of scientists. The facts appeared to remain constant—objects in the room moved about and objects not in the room at the time the seance began suddenly appeared in space. Reports were many, sometimes conflicting in detail, but the overall conclusion was that the phenomena were genuine.

The summer I saw the Schneider boys, Schrenck-Notzing was away from Munich but he agreed that I might sit with them if I took three of his committee along to verify any reports I might make. I took Reuter from Berlin, Dr. Probst and Major Kaliphas from Munich, all trained investigators. We went to the Schneider home in Braunau, an Austrian border town, later famous as the birthplace of Hitler. I took rooms at a typical village hotel and the sittings were held in my bedroom, a large room with stone walls and only one window. Since Rudi liked to work with a cabinet we devised a cabinet of sorts by stringing two blankets across the corner of the room furthest from the window. Rudi sat about 15 feet from this cabinet and one or the other of us held his hands and controlled his feet; indeed we took turns in this matter of immobilizing his hands and legs so that when we made our report no one could suggest collusion between any one of us and Rudi. The window was darkened but a good red light was on and we could see clearly.

Under these conditions I witnessed genuine physical phenomena of a remarkable sort. The blankets billowed out and sometimes flew up to the ceiling as though a great gust of wind had struck them from behind. We knew of a certainty that there was no one and nothing in the cabinet, nor any opening into the cabinet from the solid stone walls. Various toys which we had placed on a small table in front of the cabinet and directly under the light scudded across the table or picked themselves up and placed themselves down on a different part of the table. Then a small but perfectly shaped hand came from behind the blankets, moved toward me, stopped directly in front of me, took from my breast pocket a silk handkerchief and carried it back into the cabinet. A moment later the handkerchief was returned to me, by the same hand, tied in eighteen knots.

I have always considered the time and energy which went into that trip to Braunau one of my better investments for I know now that physical phenomena do occur and under the most exacting conditions. My friend Will Goldston, the magician, also witnessed Rudi's work and declared that under the same conditions a whole group of prestidigitators could not produce the phenomena which he had witnessed. In 1933, at the end of a series of test seances under direction of the Council of the National Laboratory of Psychical Research in London, Dr. Henry H. Price, editor of their bulletins, documented in detail the "absolutely genuine psychic phenomena" which were produced. In spite of all the testimony, however, and notwithstanding my long experience in the field, I am glad that I saw Rudi's work rather than taking anybody's word for it.

During the decade between 1928 and 1938 I was invited to lecture in various parts of the world. One of the more interesting trips was to Sweden and Denmark. At the Concert Hall in Stockholm I spoke to four hundred people on the subject of "Spiritualism, Science and Religion" and shared the surprise of the press that the hall was not only full but that scores were turned away. While in Scandinavia I was asked one day to give a sitting to a lady who preferred to remain anonymous. There was nothing unusual in that request, nor in having this modest and dignified lady welcome me cordially, if noncommittally, and proceed at once to the purpose of my visit—which was for me to fall asleep! Nor was I surprised when I wakened at the end of the sitting to find her very much moved by what had come to her. But I was surprised indeed when she presented me with a British Royal Signet, containing seventy-three small diamonds. The sitter was Queen Maud. Later I gave the royal signet to my second wife as a wedding present.

My scrapbooks have many clippings from German and Scandinavian newspapers and the tenor of them all is the same; it was as if a new footnote were being added to the literature on immortality, for the people themselves were participating in the proof of ongoing life.

On one trip to Europe, 1932, I decided to go around the world and see what I might turn up of interest in the psychic field. However, without introductions or even any concrete idea as to what I was looking for, I did not get much of value. Now I would know where to go and how to find what I wanted. Especially in India I expected to discover some yogin who might advance my training. What I found was that the techniques I had learned from Swami Yogananda were the ones all the others used. Moreover, the mill-run yogis looked at me strangely; did I not already produce results? What more did I want? Few of them could do as much. There were others, however, whom I sensed to be way beyond me. They were embarked on the hard course of the permanent expansion of consciousness and their disciplines reached into every facet of their life, transforming their characters. In those days I was not out to have my character transformed. So I came away from India as any other tourist might with mixed memories of beauty and degradation, not much wiser than I went.

Much the same thing happened in Egypt. I saw mediums in Cairo and Alexandria, asked my questions of the Sphinx, sensed that there was wisdom around me, but was content to accept clairvoyance for spiritual insight.

In 1937 I was invited by the Society for Psychical Research in Sydney, Australia, to give a series of lectures down under. Earlier Sir Arthur Conan Doyle had urged me to visit Australia; he himself had been so well received there, and had found able investigators.

My sailing had to be postponed several times because of a seamen's strike on the West Coast and when I finally did get passage I found the ship overcrowded with passengers eager to get home. I shared a stateroom with a Roman Catholic priest and a Sydney businessman. The priest and I were soon good friends, but the businessman was a poor traveler and very difficult to get on with. Certainly he had no interest in me. I never discuss my affairs with strangers unless there is some reason to do so and he surely expressed nothing of his interests. No one on the ship knew why I was going to Australia. But when we stopped in Auckland, New Zealand, a reporter came aboard with instructions from his paper to get an interview with me. His paper, it seemed, was owned by the same publishers who owned the Sydney *Sun*, and the *Sun* was interested in advance publicity for my Australian tour. So I talked freely with the reporter. Late that afternoon, just before we sailed, the evening edition of the paper was brought aboard. Everyone was soon reading the local paper, on the front page of which was my picture and a story about my work, with the result that the good priest dodged me for the rest of the trip while my other roommate suddenly became affable. He was a member of the Society for Psychical Research hurrying home to be on hand for the lectures of the American medium due in his country.

In Sydney I was hurried through customs and to my hotel, where I barely had time to change into dinner jacket, before I was carried off to a welcoming dinner given by the Society for Psychical Research. After the usual speeches and responses, Eric Baume, editor of the Sydney *Sunday Sun* announced that he wanted the privilege of the first private sitting with me. "We have brought Mr. Ford here at great expense," he said, "and if his tour is to be a success we will need publicity. This publicity I am able to furnish through our newspapers and radio stations. Therefore I would like a sitting about seven-thirty tomorrow morning." I easily grasped his meaning: he was not going to give me time to look him up, nor anyone else, in the Australian equivalent of *Who's Who* or to get any other information about him. He went on to say, "If this sitting is a success and I get evidential material, I will write up the whole thing in my paper. If it is a blank, I will understand and try again, for all psychics have blanks at times. But if I am convinced that Mr. Ford is not honest, we will know how to deal with the situation." He smiled at me. I know that smile. Such persons always meet me with a friendly hand extended but one eyebrow cocked, waiting for my gimmick to disclose itself. However, his precautions appeared sound to me. I have never objected to any sort of reasonable test, and as a matter of fact welcome them because test conditions not only satisfy the investigator but at the same time protect me from unfair accusations. It has always seemed to me that a psychic who refuses to cooperate in sitting under proper conditions, or one who demands to know the names of his sitters beforehand, is placing himself in a doubtful position. A psychic may get tired of all these precautions which in no way affect the discarnates intending to communicate, but they are nonetheless reasonable in our culture.

Evidently Mr. Baume received what he considered to be satisfactory material, for I was immediately asked to broadcast twice a week over the radio station controlled by his paper, and also invited to do a weekly article on psychic subjects for the paper's weekly magazine *The Woman*.

A series of four public lectures and psychic demonstrations was held in Assembly Hall. This was a large hall seating some fifteen hundred people and when I arrived for the first lecture I found a crowd milling about outside, unable to get in. Since I was alone and not recognized by anyone, my efforts to enter were protested by the crowd; who did I think I was? Jeers met the assertion that I was Arthur Ford and I was cautioned not to try that line. Finally a policeman took me in hand and was good enough to check with some of those in charge of the meeting.

At the last meeting we decided to try an experiment of broadcasting the entire procedure. In the demonstration of open clairvoyance I was to attempt to give messages not only to persons in the hall but to those listening in on the radio. Long distance telephones were installed and announcements made, asking people to call in if they received a message which particularly fitted into their context. I knew that the space-time factor has been repeatedly proved to be of no importance in psychic experiments, but still I did not know how successful this kind of experiment might prove. Certainly it was the first time it had ever been attempted.

By the time the meeting was over, seventeen persons had telephoned to verify details of messages. The next week the charming editor of *The Woman*, a Mrs. Hamilton, and a photographer traveled hundreds of miles to interview those who had telephoned their recognition of messages. Their story, which was widely reprinted, especially in England, brought the usual charges of fraud, collusion and all that. To all such response I was inured and yet it seemed a bit on the fatuous side that people should think a reliable newspaper would go to that much trouble to contrive a hoax. In all, the response by mail, most of it commendatory, was so large that we gave up attempts to include the radio audience.

Among the members of the Society for Psychical Research in Australia were men of scientific and academic standing, including Sir Ernest Fisk who had just been knighted for his work in establishing radio communications throughout the Empire. One night when I was dining with him, he suddenly asked me if there were anyone in London with whom I would like to talk. I said I would like to speak to my friend, Maurice Barbanell, editor of *Psychic News*. Almost as quickly as if it were a local call we had Barbie on the line and we talked as easily and clearly as if we were next door. This sort of communication sounds commonplace now, but even as short a time as twenty years ago it was on the unusual side.

Both in Melbourne and Brisbane I continued to speak over the radio, answering questions about survival and communication. I was supposed to give a second series of talks in Sydney before leaving the country but upon my return from Brisbane the owners of Assembly Hall refused its use for further meetings. My sponsors then took the huge Town Hall which seats thirty-six hundred people and boasts one of the greatest pipe organs in the world. For this final meeting all seats were sold out. Frankly, I was impressed because I was receiving a handsome share of the gate receipts, but on the day of the meeting a heavy storm struck Sydney and all but flooded the town. Water was standing hub-deep in the streets and I expected to be speaking to a quarter-filled house. Surprisingly the hall was packed, even standing room being sold out. Still more fortunately my clairvoyance was particularly clear and person after person rose with a gasp—or sometimes with a flood of tears—to claim some message from a departed relative, friend or acquaintance. Every now and then I myself am impressed afresh by the weight of evidence which comes through, and this last meeting in Australia was one such time.

I returned to Auckland, New Zealand, where I was sponsored by the Quest Club, and had no sooner stepped off the ship than I was taken to a radio station for an interview. As we left the station the new friend who had met me explained that we would go at once to Rota Ruri, a famous hot springs. Of course I understood the purpose of the whisking away. I was to be under surveillance and definitely out of touch with any possible source of information about local persons and their background. This was all right with me, for Rota Ruri is a fine place to rest before a demanding assignment. The surrounding country is exotic. Hundreds of geysers shoot steaming water into the air; paths meander among the geysers and signs warn the visitor not to wander off the paths for quicksands and whirlpools abound and one who slips into either is likely to be sucked down to his death.

The first afternoon I decided to take a stroll by myself, but gradually became confused as to direction and finally realized that I had not the slightest idea in which direction the hotel lay. All about the countryside were small neat cottages in which the local Maoris lived. The Maoris are the original citizens of the country, the group which superior-minded Nordics are inclined to call "the natives." In looks they are similar to Polynesians, brown of skin, tall in stature and with fine, lithe bodies. Their culture is old, their natural dignity marked. Increasingly they are part of the composite culture of New Zealand, educated in the public schools and moving into cosmopolitan life. However, in the outlying areas the older people largely speak their Maori language and continue certain distinctive customs. Religiously they are almost entirely Christians, but they have a charming folklore which their children inherit a good deal as English-speaking children take on Red Riding Hood and the Three Bears.

I knew there were Maori families living in most of the cottages and I figured that almost any individual among them could direct me to the hotel. Certainly I was not conscious of any leading as I approached a nearby cottage which appeared to be occupied. When I knocked on the door a charming Maori woman responded. "Come in, Mr. Ford," she said, "we knew you would be coming today and we're waiting for you."

May I say I was taken aback? Here I was several hours from Auckland and no one but my friend knew I was at the springs and he did not know that I had taken a stroll by myself. Entering the cottage, I found about a dozen men and women, all Maoris, waiting! They were cordial in a simple unconstrained way; none of them seemed to think it strange that I had dropped in; they were indeed waiting for me. Nor do I mean that they were consciously concentrating on steering my footsteps in their direction. They were merely waiting for an event of which they had been quietly, and psychically, apprised.

We had a delightful visit. One of the group told me several interesting things about my own affairs, one of them being that when I left New Zealand I would meet a woman who would have a good deal to do with my future life; that after leaving this island I would spend some time on another island before I returned to America, and that on that island I would make decisions that would affect my whole future. I made notes, as usual, but thought little more of the conversation.

Just as the New Zealanders were advanced politically and socially, so were they independent and intelligent in the field of psychic interests. There was excellent attendance at the meetings, discussion was animated and informed, and I was glad to be in good form so far as lectures and demonstrations were concerned.

Before I left Auckland I received a cable inviting me to visit old friends in Honolulu. I had a good many acquaintances in Hawaii for the reason that my great friend, Francis Fast, in New York City, represented the Alexander Baldwin interests and I had often helped him entertain visiting Hawaiians, many of whom became interested in psychic research. With some pleasure I cabled that I would be happy to stop in Honolulu for a few weeks.

When I sailed from Auckland on the Matson liner *Monterey*, I was surprised to discover among the passengers a woman by the name of Valerie McKeown who had been active in the Society for Psychical Research in Sydney. She was an Englishwoman by birth, the daughter of a distinguished family in London, and had married an Australian businessman who had later died in Sydney. Her sister was married to a member of the newspaper clan who owned papers in Melbourne, Australia, and in Edinburgh, Scotland. Mrs. McKeown was going to Honolulu to visit friends.

Our days at sea were pleasant and our weeks in Honolulu even more pleasant, for we found that we had several mutual friends. Hawaiian hospitality is deservedly noted. Many of our friends, all of whom seemed to become hosts, were descendants of the missionaries who first went to the islands. I think it was Edna Ferber who wrote of them that "they went to Hawaii to do good, and did *well*." Mrs. Albert Waterhouse gave a reception for me and among those present was Dr. John Tanner, one of the group to whom the Houdini code messages had come in New York several years earlier. We were flown all over the islands. It was during a visit to the lovely Kona Inn on the largest of the island group that I proposed to Valerie and was astounded to have her accept me. A year later we met in Los Angeles and were married. And so the prediction of my Maori friend came true.

Our marriage was happy. It marked the end of my wandering if not of my traveling. Valerie had two young daughters, so I soon felt like a family man. We had an unostentatious but most comfortable home in Los Angeles. Valerie enjoyed entertaining and had a gift for it. I helped to organize the Los Angeles Institute for Psychical Research, of which Hamlin Garland became president, and soon an intriguing program was under way. People from the East were constantly coming West to join in some of our ventures, or not infrequently individuals flew out for private sittings. I went on lecturing but I took more time for friends and study and personal pursuits. The old saw that "east, west, home's best" took on meaning for me.

CHAPTER 13

Catastrophe

WISER PERSONS than I have observed that success often carries at its heart the germ of defeat. The result of the publicity coming my way and the increased work which ensued was what would be expected: I got tired. Tired to the bone. Indeed, by December, 1930, I felt played out. The only thing I wanted in life was a chance to take a good rest, a chance to do nothing and gather energy again. So I decided to go to South Carolina and visit my mother and stepfather.

Leighton Thomas was a large, good-natured man, religiously an old-line Baptist, temperamentally an old-line gentleman, and conventionally uninterested in things psychic, but I always felt at ease with him. He was surprised, I believe, when he began to feel at ease with me. One day on one of my earlier trips home just before I was leaving for my second journey to England, he pointed his finger at me and said, "You were a preacher once, weren't you?" I said that I was. "But now you're not preaching any more." I said that I no longer had a church. "And you're taking off for Europe on a ship?" I said I was leaving almost immediately. He shook his head. "You'd better remember Jonah and keep off of ships." He meant what he said, too; he was definitely not joking.

I think Leighton lived and died without knowing how deep my mother's interest in my mediumship had become and how essentially a part of her religion it was. She had a gift for not annoying people with her interests which they did not share, but going right on with her interests. Years later when she knew she was going to die, it was like her to make arrangements for her funeral with her minister, who knew her as a pillar of the church, and then, after he had left her room, to turn to me with a chuckle and remark that the good man would be surprised if he knew she would be right there at the service listening to everything he said. My mother and I were friends and I looked forward to getting down there to her home for the recuperation I knew I needed.

It also happened that my younger sister Edith wanted to make a trip home. She was a member of a New York firm and had also been working hard. In fact, her work had taken its toll in the form of a spot on her lung, and since tuberculosis had caused the death of several members of our family, she had decided to move to Denver. In those days the accepted procedure for persons threatened with tuberculosis was to move west into mountain air. Naturally Edith wanted to see Mother before she left. She invited her secretary and friend, Grace Harrington, a particularly lovely young woman, to come with us.

We had just the kind of fortnight's rest we wanted. I felt made over, or at least able to face the grind of speeches and appointments with a measure of verve. The three of us were grateful and happy the day we started back to New York. Then just as we crossed the North Carolina line, the driver of an empty tobacco truck rammed into us. My sister was killed at once and Grace so seriously injured that she died three hours later. I was thrown from the car and when I regained consciousness I found that I was in Baker Sanitarium at Lumberton, North Carolina, suffering from an injured back, several crushed ribs, facial lacerations, and internal injuries. I was put in a plaster cast and the outlook for my recovery seemed dim.

My mother carried the burden of responsibility for the double funeral and for establishing responsibility for the accident. The driver had fallen asleep at the wheel, and he was indicted for manslaughter by the coroner's jury. We did not wish to prosecute him since we saw no sense in causing more sorrow. I have never felt that any sort of revenge is worth while.

Because of the recent newspaper publicity about me, the press carried the story of the accident all over the world. Hundreds of letters, telegrams and cablegrams flooded in. As I improved a bit, my mother found much amusement in the fact that before the messages were delivered to the village hotel where she was staying, news of their content and signature would already be common knowledge.

My doctor, a young chap, and a graduate of Harvard University Medical School, took note of all the publicity and told me that he was himself interested in psychic matters. One of his professors in medical school had been Dr. L. R. G. Crandon, husband of the famous Boston medium, Margery. My doctor expressed regret that I was in no shape for experimentation.

Actually I was under heavy sedation; that is, having regular injections of morphine. My most vivid memory of those first days in the hospital is of the glorious relief from pain which those shots brought me. Although I knew that narcotics and opiates of many sorts have from early times played a part in some types of psychic and religious experience, still I had never had any personal interest in experimenting with them. But there I was taking morphine and it was affecting my psychic pick-up. We discovered the fact rather incidentally.

My gentle, kindly friend, Francis Fast, whom many called Saint Francis, came down to see me. He was then living on his estate in a Jersey suburb of New York City where he conducted a small home circle devoted to the development of techniques of meditation. As always happens in such groups when properly constituted, one of the group, a schoolteacher, had developed mediumship. She had clairvoyantly picked up details about my injuries, as well as about the furnishings of my room.

No doubt this fact was in the mind of Francis Fast when he sat by me on the second night of his visit, for, although I was apparently asleep and had no knowledge or memory of his speaking to me, he asked me if I could visit his study group in New Jersey. Immediately I complied and gave him details which he was able to verify by telephone later that evening. This episode intrigued my doctor. If I could pick up happenings in New Jersey, why not right there in other rooms of the hospital. Perhaps I could tell him about other patients, check his diagnosis, tell him what he would find in operations to be performed the next day. I could. And so he began to drop into my room each night after the hospital had quieted down to give me an injection of morphine, and then make notes of what I reported. It did not occur to me that this procedure was in any way harmful. I just knew that I had to have the opiate if I were to endure the pain, and in those dark days that was all I cared about. Nor did it occur to the doctor, I feel sure, that he was doing me harm. No doubt he intended to withdraw the morphine gradually. I was a contented patient and he was an eager-minded, experimental physician.

Fortunately, after a few weeks, my mother—who had returned to her home—became concerned about the length of my stay in the hospital and consulted a cousin of mine who lived near her, an excellent physician, who knew the extent of my injuries. He felt I should be sufficiently recovered by this time to be moved home. Of course he knew nothing about the heavy sedation I was still receiving. So it was that one day my mother simply arrived at the hospital with a husky male nurse and took me home to her good care.

That afternoon my medical cousin realized that I had become the unwitting victim of morphine addiction. He explained the situation to me and made it plain that there were two methods of procedure—either gradual withdrawal, or the more drastic method of ending the use of morphine peremptorily. In either case I could expect intolerable suffering, but in the latter case it would be shorter —and far more intense. Since I was horrified at the idea of becoming, or having become, a morphine addict, and since I had to suffer in either case, I chose the short route to freedom. My cousin explained that having once chosen, there would be no turning back. At the moment I agreed but by night I was in such agony both of mind and of body that my decision was nothing to me; death and even the kind of hell my Calvinist forebears believed in seemed preferable.

To relive the next days even in memory causes the cold sweat to break out. It is said that one does not remember pain, really, but certainly one does remember nervous anguish. The old nerve paths quicken. During that time every nerve in my body shrieked convulsively. I could not eat, neither could I sleep. I wept through the days and cursed through the nights. The age-old questions seared my mind: why had I not died with the two girls? What had

God against me? Job's ancient despairing cry, "curse God and die," seemed the only logic. But I could not die, and I still clung to some sort of belief in God's justice.

The final blow came in the form of blindness. For something like three weeks I could see nothing. Moreover, when physical sight was gone, I commenced to lose hope. Had I suffered all this time merely to live in darkness the rest of my life? Why should I try to go on? Why should I live? One night when my mother had reached exhaustion almost equal to my despair, my doctor offered me a sedative. Somehow on the instant I found the strength to rise up in bed and, hitting out blindly in the dark, I struck him sharply in the face. He told me afterward that in all his practice nothing had ever made him so happy as that blow in the face.

By the time I had recovered from the need of morphine I had developed so much nervous tension that life was still not worth living. By day every noise irritated me, but instead of falling asleep when the quiet night closed in, I became more brightly, acutely awake. Nor did my sight return; I had only vague perception of forms. My doctor thought it a good idea for me to go to New York and have a round of baths and massage, as well as a change of scene and a chance to be with friends. Once there, however, my condition grew worse. I could not rest. I was deeply afraid of anything that sounded like sleeping medicine, and refused the aid of any kind of drugs.

In New York I was in the hands of a fine, reputable medical man and if in reporting these agonized days I am making him sound unresourceful, I must be overlooking some of his honest and earnest attempts to bring me relief. Finally he suggested, practically, that alcohol might break the tension. He would administer it himself.

Up to this time it had never occurred to me to drink,

although I moved in circles in which drinking was as much an accepted part of social intercourse as eating. Some of my friends laid my total abstinence to protection of my psychic gifts but in reality I was a teetotaler by what might be called inherited conviction.

We made quite an occasion of that first medicinally administered drink. We both thought that one stiff drink would be enough, but surprisingly, I seemed to have a built-in resistance to alcohol. One drink made no impression; nor two, nor three. Since the doctor was convinced that a good bout of liquor would break my nervous tension, he felt I should drink on until I gave in to the alcohol. I had finished that bottle of Scotch and part of another when finally I passed out and went to sleep. Then I slept for three days. Awakening, I found that I not only felt better, more normal, but my sight had fully returned. I was relaxed and calm. I went off to Florida for a good rest.

The doctor instructed me to continue drinking moderately until the tension was completely past. I must have been about the most tense person in the world, for it took some twenty years and a lot of suffering and humiliation before I overcame both the tension and the need of alcohol.

CHAPTER 14

Power Greater Than Myself

DURING THOSE TWENTY YEARS when I was meeting tension with alcohol, I continued to travel over the world. Much of my best work was done during this time. I was merely a social drinker, or thought I was. I failed to note that there were an increasing number of times when for days I could not work. Usually I controlled my drinking during my heavier schedules and for considerable periods would not drink at all. But I always had a subconscious date for starting again . . . after the end of this tour . . . after I have finished this engagement. Probably fifteen years went by before I looked at the fact that the periods of drinking were getting closer together, and often overlapping.

At times I tried various cures and always hopefully. So far as I know medical science has never found a cure for alcoholism. An individual can be sobered up but the problem of keeping him sober has largely eluded medicine, and, until a few years ago, had usually eluded religion. It remained for a group of alcoholics themselves, helped through the psychic insight of one of themselves, to throw a flood of light on this ancient problem. Actually I do not think I ever heard the word alcoholism, certainly not as applied to myself. A person was a drunk, a bum, a moral

weakling, an unregenerate sinner. I am sure I must have
been all of these and more; the something more was that I
was a sick man, ill with an incurable disease which could
lead only to a mental institution or an early death. Alcoholism is said to be the fourth largest killer among diseases
today.

In my dilemma my knowledge of psychic things was of
no help to me. At that time I thought of my psychic ability
as something that had come to me unsought and I resented
the fact that nearly everyone I met looked upon me as a
charlatan or a lunatic, or at best as a guinea pig to be used
for interesting experiments. To me it seemed that the facts
of ongoing life and of communication were so plain that a
person who could not see their religious significance, must
himself be mentally retarded. In our culture that made me
the odd-ball, calling the majority crazy. Even with many
Spiritualists I could not be completely at ease because they
so often appeared to tear the doctrine of survival and communication out of their setting. I blamed the stupid, scorned
the biased, and considered myself superior to both groups,
unaware that alcoholism was my response to our mutual
failures and frustration.

In the early forties my wife and I were living in California. Fundamentally we were happy; we enjoyed our
life together. In those days there were a good many interesting Britishers in California and our house was the
scene of much good conversation. Moreover, the Los
Angeles Institute for Psychical Research was vigorously
researching and I had a hand in many undertakings. I saw
a good deal of Yogananda, and great man that he was, he
gave me his continuing friendship without recrimination.
I am sure he sensed my predicament and I always felt his
understanding and compassion, but he knew I had to come
to myself; this was a path no one could travel for me. And

to me my path looked pleasant enough; certainly I did not lack for friends, comforts, nor even for money. But I seldom felt well, and I made an increasing number of trips to the hospital with a variety of ailments induced or complicated by alcohol. Also I had to cancel more lectures or go on the platform only half sober.

And then one morning I wakened in Florida without the slightest memory as to when I had left my home in California. I sought the porter and he told me that all the way across country I had remained in my room, occasionally sending for food, and that I had been very quiet, very drunk, and very absent-minded. I notified my wife of my whereabouts and she notified me that she was getting a divorce for the sake of her two young daughters. We reached a mutual agreement without rancor or bitterness. I do not blame her. I am sure that if we had known the true nature of alcoholism she would have continued to help me in the same spirit of unselfish devotion she had manifested for several years. If there is anything worse than being an alcoholic, it must be to be married to one, or to have to live in a family with one. The personality of the alcoholic changes; he becomes selfish, undependable. Then there is simultaneous physical deterioration.

After our separation I gave up my work for long periods, went to New York and took other jobs, but then I would have lucid periods and decide I was over the worst and go back to the lecture platform again. Finally in 1946 I decided to leave everything and everybody that had ever meant anything to me, go down to Florida and fight out my battle. I went to Florida all right and I fought, but it was a losing battle. People speak of alcoholics' falling in the gutter or winding up on the Bowery, but the gutter is not always a place; it can be a state of mind. And "skid row" is not always the back street of some city; it is something an alcoholic carries around in his consciousness. I know that one can lie in the gutter while sleeping in his own house, and I wound up on my own skid row while living in a luxury hotel. Unfortunately, perhaps, I always had enough money to see me through bad times and I had many loyal friends, most of whom finally got fed up and gave up—for which I do not blame them.

In 1949 I entered the hospital again, not because of acute alcoholism but because of a complete physical breakdown. Comparatively few people actually die of alcoholism; they die of other diseases brought on by the prolonged malnutrition which accompanies alcoholism. It was while in this hospital that I had a psychic vision which made a deep impression upon me, but it did not effect its transforming work for some months.

When I was released I was told that I would have to accept invalidism and probably had not long to live. If I ever drank again I would be authorizing my own death. Although I had never been afraid of death, the vividness of my own psychic experience made me realize that after death I would experience no happier state of consciousness than I deserved.

At this point I tried to help myself. Having studied yoga and having read widely in occultism and metaphysics, I knew all the theories but had never applied their more demanding aspects to myself. Now I understood that I had better use whatever I knew for my own healing. So I began a belated attempt to change my mental attitude and remake my body. By May of 1950 I had been sober for four months, not because I enjoyed being sober but because I was trying to demonstrate some of the psychic laws I knew. They were working. I felt better than in years. My psychic gifts were again in full force. I accepted a lecture contract which was to begin in June. I went to New York.

One night I happened to meet my friend Cliff B——
who had become interested in psychic matters a few years
previous when I had happened to pick him out of an audience to give him an evidential message. Cliff invited me to
dinner and as we dined he mentioned that he was going to
a meeting of a group in which he was interested; the most
interesting discussion group he knew anything about. He
invited me to go with him and I accepted. So we went to
the Parish House of the Church of the Heavenly Rest on
upper Fifth Avenue where a couple hundred happy-look-
ing people had gathered. I recognized a few old friends.
And then I discovered that all these people had once been
the victims of alcoholism. Previously I had not even known
that Cliff had once been an alcoholic. I listened with interest to what one and another said about their past suffering and degradation; they spoke a language I knew too
well. This was the first time I ever heard alcoholism discussed as a "physical allergy with a mental compulsion";
they were talking about the treatment of a disease rather
than dealing with unredeemable moral weakness. I got a
terrific spiritual lift from that meeting; the sincerity and
complete humility of the people who spoke deeply impressed me. This was group therapy at its best. Nevertheless, I felt on the outside because I had already conquered
my drinking—I thought. I had passed beyond need of their
therapy.

A short time afterward I wakened in a strange hotel
room and to my horror realized that I had been drunk for
more than a week. One of the symptoms of alcoholism is
the blackout, a condition in which the victim seems to be
in a state of normal consciousness but has no memory of
having taken a drink. It is almost as if an invading entity
had taken over, worked his havoc, and then left when he
was satiated. I lay in my bed sunk in the realization that I

had reached the saturation point with alcohol and that the time had come to start the agonizing process of straightening out again. I knew what the experience involved—the suffering, both physical and mental; the remorse and shame. I wanted to call my New York doctor but the last time he had seen me through a severe bout he had told me that medicine could do no more for me and that if I ever drank again he intended to commit me to an institution for a year. I had no heart for calling a strange doctor who would demand tests and probably hospitalization for the genuine illness which returned with the use of alcohol. So for eighteen hours I fought out my despair alone. I sank into a depression so dreadful that early the second morning, around two o'clock, it seemed to me the only desirable outcome was death. The logical thing, I decided, was to go ahead and let this binge be the last one. I would just drink myself out. I reached for the telephone to call room service.

And in the reaching an odd thing happened.

I knocked the Gideon Bible off the table. Automatically I picked it up from the floor and a memory of something I had often done as a child came to me. Back then I used to open the Bible at random, run my finger along a page and stop; whatever phrase my finger touched was my "fortune" for the day. This time the phrase at which my finger stopped was the seventh verse of the first chapter of Second Timothy—"for God hath not given us the spirit of fear; but of power, and of love, and of a sound mind."

Could God have spoken to my need more clearly?

Then my eye caught sight of a pamphlet which had been lying under the Bible ever since the night I had come in from that meeting with Cliff. I remembered vaguely that those recovered drunks had said they would go at any time, day or night, to help another drunk who had reached bottom. I pulled myself up on my pillow. They *had* said it. Still, it didn't make sense. I lay back and pondered. My address book also lay on the telephone stand; there were the names of many friends, good friends. But if I called any one of them he would say, "You're drunk; roll over and sleep it off and I'll see you tomorrow." Why should these strangers do what a friend would probably refuse? When one loses faith in himself he also loses faith in others; cynicism and a deep distrust of other people's motives are symptoms of alcoholism. The habitual drunk has tried everything and found it wanting. Still, there was the telephone number on the pamphlet; the number to be called in need.

I dialed and in twenty minutes two men walked into my room. They were relaxed, friendly, completely without recrimination. One of them remarked that I was on the edge of DTs and gave me a shot of whiskey. The other chuckled softly and told me he knew all the landmarks in this place of despair; he had been there. And the tale he told me, briefly, simply, was more shocking than my own. Both men seemed to take it for granted that I was going to come to myself by means of the Power which they themselves had laid hold on. As they talked I grew more calm inwardly. At least I was able to listen, although half of my attention was riveted on the dreadful moment when they would walk out of the room to go to work and I would again be alone.

But they did not leave me alone. A telephone call brought two other men walking into the room before the first two left. They also were relaxed, confident and willing to share what they had found. For once I was not telling them anything. I was listening. So it went for three days and nights; they never left me alone. Finally I quit looking for the gimmick—what *they* were going to get out of helping *me*. I would just have to believe that there were people like this. As one after another told me his story— and some of the stories were more lurid than my own—I saw that there was a pattern in their experience. It was the pattern of my own experience. The third day it suddenly dawned on me that Paul knew what he was talking about when he said that faith is the substance of things hoped for. Faith had to be my next step—faith that there was this "Power greater than myself" they kept talking about.

It was plain enough they meant God, although they did not use the term. But I told myself that I already knew about God and I had tried before to pray to Him. Now I understood that I did not know how to pray. I had never really had faith. These men in their own persons were the evidence of faith in "things hoped for"; they had been re-made; they had health and peace of mind; they had jobs and the respect of their friends; they had the love of their families. They were normal! No, they were more than normal. They had an overflow of certainty, of humility, of joy. They had triumphed through tribulation, and they were out to share.

At the same time that they were talking about unseen certainties, they were not making my way ahead sound easy or soft. I had to become completely honest; I had to make a thorough and fearless inventory of myself. In the most ruthless manner I had to write down everything that was gnawing at me; everything that appeared a frustration, a defeat; everything that made me angry, despondent, ir-ritated. And not only did I have to dig out these negative attitudes but I had to pin them onto the people and situa-tions I had been rebelling against. I had to know what I had been trying to escape from. Obviously in the process of constantly escaping from the unmanageable aspects of my life, I had hurt many people. So I also had to list the peo-ple and the harm I had done them. And then I had to go to them and make whatever amends were possible. This seemed the most impossible task, for I knew I had harmed so many, caused so much heartache, alienated so many who had tried to be my friends, and in some cases had been the means of their defeat and frustration.

In the ensuing months I tried to do all of these things. First I talked over my past with one friend; I got out everything of which I was ashamed, everything for which I was sorry. Then I went to work on the business of making amends. Never once did I meet with rebuff from an individual of whom I honestly asked forgiveness. The tragedy was that there were some I could not find.

The Power greater than myself was real! Nearer than breathing, closer than hands and feet—how often I had read those words but never taken them in.

Soon I was attending meetings where other recovered drunks met in a fellowship that is like no other fellowship on earth. These people understood each other. In the firsthand stories of degradation and restoration I began to take in what was meant by the grace of God. I could not explain what had happened to me but like the blind man by the gate who had his sight restored by Jesus, I knew whereas I had been blind, now I could see. There was much gratitude and humility in the group. And always, of course, new people who needed help.

Throughout the following months I watched my own resurrection. I know that spiritual healing takes place because I have had a rebirth to health. I know that fear can change to faith, humiliation to humility, shame to assurance, but fellowship is essential if one is to consolidate the gains of any spiritual experience.

In the process of remaking my life I did some thinking about my own peculiar gifts. But again one does not weigh and ponder abstractly; he has to work out his attitudes in action. Although I returned to old activities, so far as mediumship was concerned, I began to work from a new point of view.

CHAPTER 15

Life with Dimension

As I WENT about the business of scrutinizing my past and trying to make amends as I could to people who had been hurt or harmed by my alcoholism, I found myself wondering if the whole process were not a good deal like the Judgment which is said to be meted to each soul after death. Every day new insights came to me; sometimes a frightening disclosure. Nothing I had done was without meaning.

But not all the disclosures were disquieting. Occasionally I saw that I had influenced a life for good, giving new energy to some disheartened individual. However, this change of attitude had come not from but through me. I was astounded that anyone who had been as large a failure as I considered myself, could have done as much good, even though that good was relatively inconspicuous. Certainly I was reappraising myself and in the process my own personality began to change.

Often my mind went back to a psychic experience I had had when I lay desperately ill in a veterans' hospital in Coral Gables. At that time it had impressed but not changed me, but now it began to take hold. What precipitated my acute illness I have forgotten, but I was in a critical condition and my friends were told that I would probably not live through the night. I did not know the verdict, of course, but when I heard a doctor say to a nurse, "Give him the needle, he might as well be comfortable," I surmised that this was *it* and I wondered how long it would take to die, but my only emotion was one of hazy curiosity.

Then I realized that I was floating in the air above my bed. I saw my body but it did not interest me. I felt at peace; indeed, peace is too hackneyed a term for my deep feeling that everything was as it should be. Then I was unconscious. Or rather, after a time which had no feeling of time at all, I knew that I had been unconscious, but that now I was floating through space with no sense of a body and yet as my full and complete *self*. I saw that in some way I had reached a green valley with mountains on every side, and everywhere a brilliance of light and color such as I had never experienced before. Coming toward me were people and I realized that they were all friends and acquaintances I had thought of as dead. Yet here they were. I seemed to be recognizing them by their personality traits rather than by their customary "looks" for I was aware that some who had died in decrepit old age now gave the impression of vigorous youth. Two cousins who had died in early childhood were now mature; that is, they were complete personalities. I did not question the absence of the marks of former physical identity because I knew each one satisfactorily for just what he was; there was no veil of flesh between us.

Seeing one old friend I would be reminded of another and note that he was not present. Finally I asked about a few whom I missed. No one answered, but a blur seemed to come over my eyes. I knew I was in the same spot but the light grew dim and the colors lost their brilliance; those to whom I had been speaking faded out while those of whom I had inquired appeared in hazy shapes. I grew heavy; my thoughts shot out to former earthly pursuits and I realized, without knowing why, that I was being allowed to view a lower sphere. I cried out to the friends for whom I had asked and I felt they heard but they did not answer. Then everything cleared again and a gentle radiant personality stood beside me, smiling. "Do not worry about them. They can come here any time they want to, if they desire it more than anything else." My concern for them gave way to an unanxious state.

Everyone around me seemed busy. Without knowing what they were doing, I knew that their activity was good and right, and I saw that they were very happy. Some to whom I had been bound by close ties in the past did not now pay much attention to me, but I did not resent their inattention. Others whom I had known slightly—and some I had not known at all—seemed attracted to me. I knew without explanation that some law of affinity was at work.

At one point—all this went on without any sense of time—I found myself standing before a beautiful building of gleaming, dazzling white such as I had never before imagined. I knew without being told that this was the Judgment Hall; I knew, too, that I was to wait in a huge anteroom. I heard voices and through the wide doorway I glimpsed two long tables with people sitting at them. They were talking about me. So this was the judgment! Words came back to me, "The day of the Lord cometh like a thief in the night."

As I waited I began to review my life. It was not a happy process. Then I sensed that the people at the long tables were also taking inventory of my life. However, the incidents that gave me concern did not seem to worry them. Their categories of sin were not those of the Baptist Church of my youth: alcoholism, sex, and what are called worldly pursuits. Rather, they spoke over and over of selfishness, egotism, stupidity, and frequently used the word dissipation, but not in reference to dissoluteness; they were speaking of the dissipation of energy, gifts, opportunities. They brought to light selfish stupid acts of my youth which I had long since pushed out of consciousness and at the same time they smiled over some of the simple kindly acts such as any man does for others and promptly forgets. Obviously, they were trying to establish the main trend of my life.

Indicating me, one spoke of my having failed to accomplish "what he knew he had to finish." I gathered that I had been born into the world with some well-defined plan or purpose, and that I had somehow either failed to accept my destiny or had not matured to the point of knowing what it was that I had to do.

The word "record" was used many times. I felt as if I must have been equipped with a built-in tape recorder upon which every experience and attitude had made an indelible impression. I wanted to hear the whole record and yet I seemed to know that they were not going to let me sense more than the life immediately past, lest my attention be drawn from the task at hand. As I stood alone—very much alone—before the open door of this Judgment Hall, I was not then analyzing what I was experiencing; I was only experiencing.

Then all at once I sensed that they were deliberating sending me back to earth to finish my assignment, and I rebelled completely. Definitely I did not relish the thought of taking on the beaten diseased body I had left in the hospital. However, they were not asking my permission; they were not consulting me. I saw another door before me and some way I knew that if I passed through that door I would be back in my bed. My earth nature reasserted itself. Like a spoiled child having a tantrum, I pushed my feet against that door and fought against its being opened. I can remember using rather violent language. Then I had a sudden sense of hurtling through space. I opened my eyes —and looked into the face of the nurse.

Afterwards the nurse told me that during the time I had been in coma I had not moved nor given any trouble at all, but for half an hour or so before I regained consciousness I struggled and shouted invectives, insisting to someone that I did not want to wake up. Knowing the nurse, I did not explain. What could I say that would persuade her or anyone else that I had experienced a reality beyond any I had known in all my previous years?

Even now that I have written out the happening as simply as I can, I feel something of Paul's sense of futility. For his experience of life beyond this earth he used the word "unutterable"—and I guess that is as good as any word. I was like a man once blind who miraculously regained his sight and then tried to explain an El Greco painting to those still blind. As Sidney Lanier wrote in "The Marshes of Glynn" when he was dying of tuberculosis—

> . . . belief overmasters doubt, and I know that I know. . . .
> And my spirit is grown to a lordly great compass within.

During those early post-alcoholic days this experience was vivid in my consciousness so that I understood in an entirely nontheological way that my sins were recorded against me and that sin was a different thing than I had previously supposed; also that every genuine attempt to live up to my own best insight was registered on my behalf. The vision comforted me even when it rose most brightly to rebuke me.

Also during the post-alcoholic months when I was trying to effect restitution I often thought how fortunate I was to be able to adjust relationships while still in my physical body. There are actually things that can be done better on earth than in heaven! And yet I was not trying to make headway in the present in order to save myself future heartache; I was not trying to save myself anything.

Some persons who have had a seance with me have reported that discarnate friends of theirs have also mentioned the experience of the judgment. For instance, a friend of the late John Chambers told me about a sitting he had with me in which John commented on the circumstances of his own death. John concluded, "In a way there is not as much difference between the two lives as you might expect, except that on earth you can grow and develop as you *will* to do, in a way that we cannot." Then later he commented, "It rather looks to me as if we are judged less by individual acts, or the accumulation of them, than by the slant of our lives, the goal we kept ourselves headed toward." Laughing, he added, "I don't know why I say this, though, because I haven't been judged yet."

Apparently, judgment is both a constant process and a final reckoning. It looks as if some kind of casting of the balance goes on constantly, throughout every individual's earth life, on through the interim periods when the soul may have other experiences in other dimensions of consciousness, throughout the next earth life—if there is another—and so on. No two souls make the same journey. But the goal is perfection, no less; the full realization of the individual potential, the true maturity in which the self-will is fused with the will of God. The weighing and measuring is a constant process and at any time the individual has access to knowledge of the sum which is being cast if he wants it badly enough to be still and let it come through to his self-conscious mind. There is never a time when we do not have access to knowledge of our own spiritual bank balance. In a sense the bookkeeping appears to be automatic; and yet no man is on his own in an automatic universe.

However, there are indeed judges. In a sitting someone asked if the judges were discarnates who had fulfilled their earth obligations and come to an high estate of knowledge. The answer was that the judges had never been incarnated on earth, that they are "servants of the Most High," who have not needed that discipline. Apparently "the judgment," meaning the reckoning up of a lifetime just finished, takes place when the discarnate one is ready; when he is fully conscious of his estate and aware of his own past record.

It also appears that after death many persons simply sleep for an indefinite period. If there has been a long and devastating illness the mind may need long repose. Friends who come to Fletcher asking for a loved one who has recently died are often told, "He is still sleeping." Persons killed by violence seem especially to need this sleep. The prayer book petition to be delivered from sudden death has its basis in a psychological reality; the hurtling into a new dimension without time for the ordered separation of the spiritual from the physical may be a traumatic experience unless the individual is brought gradually to consciousness of his new estate. Some individuals wish to sleep; they do not want to face whatever reckoning lies before them.

Apparently, however, the sleeping dead can be wakened to their new reality by the loving prayers of the living; indeed it seems that they are often more easily reached by a living person than by a discarnate.

It also seems plain that discarnates often cling to their earth interests with remarkable tenacity; vaguely they know they are not as before but they go on acting as if they were. This is an unhappy state. It may indeed be hell. A murderer may continue to struggle to elude his pursuers, haunted, fearful, hungry, deserted by his friends. A tyrant may still be giving orders and may still hold in bondage other discarnates who were once his henchmen and accomplices. Terrorists who worked together on earth tend to cohere as a discarnate group and to continue in terror in their own consciousness. The mind may continue to rivet attention on action for the purpose of excluding appraisal.

Persons who do not believe in ongoing life appear to have a slower wakening than persons who understand that life goes on. Moreover, those who have never believed in immortality have a devastating feeling of unreality: they know they are alive but their former earth associates do not respond to their attempts at communication. The mind skilled in concentration of the sort used in meditation seems to make the most immediate and serene adjustment to the new condition.

An instance of immediate awareness of the new state was reported to me by friends whom I shall call William and Portia. Their story really began in a previous sitting of a friend of theirs when Fletcher suddenly announced, "There's an old man here who wants to be heard. He hasn't been here long and he doesn't know how to communicate; he talks too fast. But he wants to get a message to his daughter-in-law, Portia. He says you know Portia. He is William's father. He was a doctor. He wants you to give Portia and William his love and try to get them to come here tomorrow. He stresses tomorrow."

It was three or four days before the couple were reached by telephone and when the friend had finished reporting the message there was a moment's silence at the other end of the line. Then Portia said, "William's father died last Sunday in Norway and news of his death had not even been given to the press. In fact we were out of town and did not get the word immediately ourselves."

More to please the friend than because of any belief on his own part, William made an appointment with me. On Sunday, a week after his father's death, he and Portia came. No sooner had Fletcher arrived than he reported that the father was waiting in great excitement to speak to them. Then followed an account of the father's death: he had seen too many others die with awareness that they were being met, he said, to doubt that life went right on. "So I took it in stride and came right across. I was unconscious only a few moments; everyone has a few moments of unconsciousness, I guess. Like a swift sleep."

William asked if his father had received his letter before he died and the old doctor answered, "They read it to me. They thought I was unconscious but decided to try reading the letter anyway." Whereupon he discussed the contents of the letter. He also told about William's mother who was waiting for him and their joy in being in close companionship—"although of course we had never been separated." Fletcher commented on the number of children around the father, which was not surprising, Portia explained, because the old doctor had aided scores of orphans. A long conversation went on among the three of them, via Fletcher, and many pertinent family matters were discussed. The old doctor said to his son, "The reason I wanted you to come Wednesday was because that was your birthday and I thought the best present I could give you was to send you my love firsthand."

From the information that has come to me through the years from about as many discarnates as I have acquaintances on this earth, I deduce one fact that seems to me more significant than any other—except the basic fact that life does go on. That is, that the quality of life after death is determined by the quality of life before death.

Slowly it also came to me, in the days of my own reconstruction, that the important thing about my life on this earth was that it was possible to have a present quality beyond anything I had imagined. It was now that I lived in an unobstructed universe; it was now that my thoughts outspanned communication in words; it was now that I could call upon the resources of invisible as well as visible friends. The abundant life began to take on form and meaning.

CHAPTER 16

Everyone Is Psychic

THE REACH of the mind which we call paranormal or psychic seems to me to have a good deal to do with life's dimension. We can live constricted lives, limited in our comprehension to sensory experience, or we can learn to see through and beyond appearances. This wider comprehension is thrust upon us after death but it lies within our power now. However, not everyone appears to be psychic. I used to ponder this fact. If the psychic faculty is so immensely useful, why is it not a common endowment? My conclusion was that it is more common than we realize and that everyone is at least potentially psychic.

Of course others had reached this conclusion before me. William James once remarked that the most amazing thing about psychic phenomena is their commonness. Then certainly the second amazing thing is their variance. When I began to pigeonhole the experiences I daily observed, and had, this fact was brought home to me.

First, because commonest, are the instances of psychic or paranormal cognition. It was F. W. H. Myers who first categorized the psychic states with any sharpness. William James also once remarked of him, "Whatever the judgment of the future may be on Myers' speculations, the credit will always remain to them of being the first attempt in any language to consider the phenomena of hallucination, automatism, double personality, and mediumship as connected parts of one whole subject."

Related to this attempt was the gathering of material on the communication of ideas from one mind to another without the customary channels and codes, for which he invented the term telepathy. Almost everyone has had some experience which appears telepathic. Just yesterday I picked up the phone to call a friend and while I was waiting for the operator to answer, my friend began to talk; her impulse to call me had coincided so exactly with mine to call her that I had answered the phone before it rang. Such experiences are too common with me to admit coincidence as an explanation. I have found that with certain persons I can frequently get an idea to them simply by concentrating upon a sharp image of the individual I wish to reach while saying very succintly, although voicelessly, what I want to communicate, and then putting the idea out of my mind without anxiety. Recently I needed to reach my nephew in this fashion, wanting him to call me —since I did not know where to call him. My objective was complicated by my having to impress him with the particular place I wished him to call. He called me—somewhat mystified as to why he was calling!

In group telepathy the message broadcast by one person is likely to be received in slightly varying forms by the designated recipients. For instance, William Button, then president of the American Society for Psychical Research, once asked four mediums in different parts of the country to try to pick up the image he would be telepathically broadcasting at four o'clock on a given afternoon. We all turned our expectation, so to speak, in his direction and I was impressed to record, "I'm no big shot" or "Button is a big shot." Another medium felt impelled to pick up his small son's toy gun and shoot at the toy target. Button had picked up a shotgun and taken aim in shooting position.

The literature on telepathy is not inconsiderable and some of it is extremely well documented.

Clairvoyance is one of the more common psychic experiences: discerning objects, symbols, persons, scenes, as having objective reality, although they are not within range of the ordinary senses.

One of the famous historical examples of clairvoyance is Emanuel Swedenborg's description of a great fire in Stockholm while he was visiting with friends some three hundred miles away. In the midst of their conversation he suddenly grew pale and began to describe the fire raging in Stockholm and then after a time grew calm, announcing, "Thank God, the fire is extinguished the third door from my home." Two days later letters confirmed every detail. Immanuel Kant was among the many deeply impressed by the investigation and testimony regarding the incident, for Swedenborg was one of the highly respected scholars of his day.

In our day Dr. J. B. Rhine of Duke University and his associates have conducted and tabulated thousands of experiments in clairvoyance. Using random sampling of all ages and many occupations, he has tested the ability of individuals to "see" the symbols on cards which are shuffled and turned up by controlled apparatus beyond the range of their eyes—indeed in a different room from the one in which the percipient is naming the cards. He has found in many persons an ability to name the symbols far above the range of chance.

Some students of clairvoyance like to categorize the types. So-called X-ray clairvoyance is the ability to see through opaque materials such as sealed envelopes, wooden

boxes, brick walls, et cetera. This is the kind of clairvoyance often displayed in theaters. When I put my mind
to it, I do not find it difficult to demonstrate this knack
but it has never interested me.

Traveling clairvoyance happens to me occasionally.
This is the ability to perceive something which is actually
and at the moment transpiring over a distance. Recently
while in New York I saw an incident transpiring in my
home in Florida; the incident had no particular significance
but it was substantiated as to details and time.

Louis Anspacher, lecturer and dramatist, told me that
he once fulfilled a dinner obligation at a time when he was
loath to leave his wife at home because she was ill and he
did not trust her to stay in bed as ordered by her doctor.
While dining with Belasco he suddenly saw her walking
across her room at home. Immediately he rang her up and
found that she had indeed done exactly as he had visualized
her doing. This sort of experience may be disconcerting to
the one perceived; he feels that he is living in a glass house.

Medical clairvoyance, the ability to see the internal
pattern of the human body, to identify disease and assign
its cause, is beyond me. Some clairvoyants diagnose while
awake, gathering their impressions from the patient's aura,
or seeing the body as transparent. Some are able to diagnose
in hypnotic sleep. Edgar Cayce was particularly adept at
medical clairvoyance which was at the same time traveling
clairvoyance; but then he was probably the most gifted
man, psychically, whom I have ever known. Apart from
being impressed by his diagnostic ability, people were
struck by the clairvoyance displayed in his side remarks,
readily verified. While he was in Virginia Beach, for instance, he commented on the setting of the home of a
patient in Nebraska, both the patient and the place unknown to him. "Beautiful tree in the yard; a tremendous

oak." Of a man in California, "The man isn't here yet; he's coming up on the elevator." Of a woman in Georgia, "It's a long walk out here; must be four miles; four and a quarter, really, from town."

When not in trance, Cayce diagnosed from the patient's aura, and very accurately, too. Clairvoyants who see the aura feel that they are seeing it with their ordinary eyesight. "I *see* it; that's all there is to it; it is *there.*" But some see it quite as well with their eyes closed, although they still perceive the experience as sight. From this display of light-color-energy they can not only read the condition of a subject's health, but pick up emotional disturbance and even detailed emotional problems; even read what they feel to be the spiritual pattern of the individual.

That people do indeed have auras I must attest because I, too, often see them. I do not mean that when an individual walks into the room I always see his aura as plainly as I see his body and features, but if I try to pick up the aura I usually get it, and often I get it without trying.

The true nature of the aura is a subject for investigation and currently some serious attempt is being made to measure and chart this emanation. One excellent scientist, formerly an official of the Radio Corporation of America, writes that he had been able to define the limits of the aura by instrument and that he sometimes found it recapitulating itself above the body for as high as thirty feet, as if the patterned energy were echoing at different octaves.

There is even an alphabet of the aura, so to speak, for sensitives of many centuries and many climes, as well as of many cultures, have interpreted given colors as depicting given conditions of health or emotional slant. All appear to agree, for instance, that the white light perceived around the head of certain persons is indicative of a highly developed spiritual nature. Hence the nimbus which the old masters painted around the heads of the saints.

That the gift of seeing auras is common there can be no doubt. Offhand I can name thirty persons who habitually see auras, and also two persons who are trying to perfect a method of photographing them. If the color is "out there" around the subject, then the camera should be able to record it; if it is subjective in the sense of being perceived as color when actually it is some other kind of wave translated in the sensitive's mind as color, then photography would be out of the question.

The ability to read the past lives of a subject may be related to aura reading, but certainly it is a psychic faculty very hard to document. First of all, it presupposes that most individuals have had past lives on this earth. In essence this is the theory of reincarnation; individuals must in the long stretch of time realize the full capacity of their nature, and to reach that perfection is the work of many earth experiences. The theory seems plausible to me because it accounts for the apparent unfairnesses into which many human beings are born. According to this theory the character-development process of sowing and reaping—a process with which we are familiar enough on a day-by-day basis—goes on for a span longer than one lifetime. At birth, then, individuals are given, or they make, the opportunity which offers them their best chances for growth. But I do not hold that acceptance or rejection of reincarnation markedly affects our immediate problems. The one who rejects reincarnation can become a saint quite as readily—and with the same difficulty—as the one who accepts the longer-than-one-life span.

I know fakes in this field of reading past lives; persons of some psychic ability who can concoct a fancy story about the past of any individual who comes to them. And why do I call them fakes since I cannot disprove their findings? Because they assign relatively the same past to different individuals, because they are inaccurate in depicting historical periods, but basically because they are not able to diagnose a present psychological predicament. A knowledge of past lives is useful only if it sheds light on a present entaglement of personalities who have worked on common problems in other circumstances, or illumines a present difficulty.

In the hearing of voices not audible to the ear, the voice may appear to be the very tone and accent of a person not present. For instance, when I have been in New York I have heard my mother speak in South Carolina. Checking with her, I have found that she was there; she did say what I thought she was saying at the time I thought she was speaking to me, but patently the vibrations produced by her vocal chords could not have reached me by normal auditory receiving apparatus. Was I catching her thought telepathically and imagining her voice? Perhaps so, although I felt as if I heard her in the usual manner. However, the characteristic voice so heard may be the voice of one now dead; since my mother's death I have also heard her speak to me in her own voice, and have heard the voices of others I knew well.

But clairaudience may also be the perception of a voice not distinguished by its tone or cadence and yet known to be coming from a specific individual. A woman says, "My father told me"—and she knows it was her father, but when asked if she actually heard his voice she has to say, "It was father speaking; the vocabulary is distinctively his, as you can see from my transcription; but the words came voicelessly." Those who have had the same experience—and they are legion—know exactly what she means. Often, however, the words heard inwardly do not appear to be said by some definite individual. They may be quite impersonal but spoken with authority.

The Bible contains numerous incidents of clairaudience.

For example, in II Kings 6:12, it is reported to the King of Syria, "but Elisha, the prophet who is in Israel, tells the king of Israel the words that you speak in your bedchamber." The fifth, sixth and seventh chapters of Second Kings are a history of psychic phenomena if ever one was recorded. Again in First Samuel, the third chapter, young Samuel heard a voice which he took to be Eli's but which Eli, apprised of the call, felt to be the voice of the Lord. Instead of ignoring the voice because it could not be "real," young Samuel responded as instructed by Eli, "Speak, Lord, for thy servant heareth." This is not to imply that the impersonal voice heard by so many is necessarily the voice of the Lord, but many have found that the voice which admonishes them on waking or in times of need is a dependable voice.

For instance, Socrates spoke often of his *daemon* who had guided him at crisis points in his life. Whenever he was about to take a wrong turn, his daemon spoke a restraining nay. After Socrates was sentenced to death by the Athenian court, when his friends begged him to flee the city, his response was that in accepting his sentence his daemon did not say *nay* and he therefore took it to be the better part that he should drink the hemlock as decreed.

The voices which directed Joan of Arc are as well known as the story of the girl's spectacular leadership and cruel death. In the eighteenth century, William Cowper was noted for his clairaudient powers and testified that he had heard voices describing in advance of their occurrence the most important events in his life. Many persons of genius report this experience, but so do many of lesser endowment.

Not all clairaudient experiences have significance, and it is a mistake to try to read significance into them just because they are paranormal. One day I was alone in my

Florida house, taking a nap, when I was annoyed and puzzled to hear bits of an indistinct conversation going on right there in the living room where I was asleep. Finally I realized, drowsily, that I was having a clairaudient experience. Listening more intently, I became aware that one voice was a stranger's and the other my own. And yet I heard clearly only incoherent words, such as "business" ... "contractor" ... "sign" ... and others. Then an order came from the second voice, "Wake up, Arthur. There's a man approaching the house!" I awoke abruptly, jumped up and put on a robe and was combing my hair when the doorbell rang. There stood a roofing contractor, soliciting business. As my roof was in good condition my first impulse was to berate him for disturbing my nap. However, since he had been a part of my clairaudient experience, I thanked him and took his card—and heard myself promising to call him later, probably after the next hurricane.

The Cincinnati *Post* once carried a story about a clairaudient experience I had while in that city. I had left a call at my hotel, the Gibson, for 8:00 A.M. on Monday, but I wakened a little before that time and lay listening for the phone. It rang and I was told that it was eight o'clock. Then just as I hung up the receiver I heard a voice telling me that my Uncle John had died earlier that morning. I had no Uncle John, but in my New York apartment building was a fine old gentleman whom I called Uncle John. The more I thought of the message the more concerned I became, so I called my home in New York and asked if there was anything wrong with Mr. Riley. The answer was that he had died at 1:45 A.M. and that they were just preparing to wire me. When a Cincinnati reporter heard of the incident he wired the New York *Telegram* and asked if a John Riley had died at St. Luke's Hospital and at what time. The *Telegram* replied that he had died at 1:00 A.M. The reporter then asked me for a signed order giving him permission to check on my recent incoming and outgoing telegrams and long-distance calls. When his investigation convinced him that I had received no word about Uncle John, except psychically, he wrote his story on clairaudience.

Incidents of precognition, or foreknowledge, crowd my pen. A woman who lived in a city where she had never seen a squirrel dreamed she was bitten by a mad squirrel and so reported her dream; a few days later a mad squirrel dashed out of the nowhere and bit her, and she was given rabies shots. A man, awake, suddenly saw himself taking a trip in a Pullman car with a peculiar name, an albino porter and a flag draped across one window. A few days thereafter he unexpectedly took the trip and the details were as he had seen them.

I myself have had a good many precognitive experiences, especially in dreams. In fact I am inclined to believe that about 25 per cent of our dream material is precognitive but fragmented and inaccurate in detail so that the elements of precognition fail to register unless we are keeping track of our dreams and observing their relevancy.

In trance I sometimes have precognitive clairvoyance not present in the waking state. The other day a man wrote to me that he had never ceased to be grateful to Fletcher because in the midst of the depression when he was on relief Fletcher had told him to get a job with an insurance agency, insisting that he had talent in that line and would soon work himself up in the organization. It was a field the man had never considered. But he got the job, worked up, has enjoyed every year of his work and now considers himself a wealthy man both as to money and personal satisfaction.

Postcognition is a more rare faculty than precognition in my observation, but I have met several persons who have had postcognitive experiences. Two men riding across the

open stretches of Nebraska suddenly saw Indians in full
war regalia; so plain were the Indians that they each
ejaculated aloud and simultaneously pointed out a window. A second later there were no Indians; other passengers looking out the windows had not seen them. But
the conductor attested that the spot had been a former
Pawnee camping ground some seventy-five years previous;
he had the tale from his grandfather. . . . A friend saw a
ship sinking in mid-ocean. Patently there was no ship, but
he was able to describe it in detail and persistent investigation disclosed that a ship of that description had disappeared in a waterspout at about that place.

Some dreams impart information in a roundabout way.
For instance, in the days when I drank more than I should
I often mislaid money. On one occasion a hundred dollar
bill was missing. I felt sure it was in my hotel room but
where I had hid it I could not imagine. That night I had
such a sharp dream of an acquaintance named George
Baker that in the morning I decided to call him. Picking
up the Manhattan telephone directory I hunted the name
and there between the pages listing Bakers was my hundred dollar bill. A neat device of the subconscious.

My friend Louise Richardson had a dream of similar
nature. She wears a ring composed of three separate circles
of gold, the two outer rings set with rubies and the central and larger ring set with pearls. At night she places them
in a row on her dresser. One morning the pearl circlet was
missing, although the other two lay in their customary
places. No one but her husband had been in the apartment
and he knew he had not touched the rings. She was beside
herself for several days for the rings were heirlooms and
irreplaceable. And then one night she dreamed of a handsome boy, perhaps twelve years old. She asked his name and
he replied that it was Hassett. When she asked where he

lived he said he did not know the number but his place was on the northwest corner of Fitzgerald Avenue in Rugby. She wakened and pondered. She knew no one by the name of Hassett. She did know a suburb called Rugby back in her home city but no Fitzgerald Avenue. Finally she went for the telephone book. The metropolitan Chicago directory was on a low shelf between the suburban and classified directories. She looked up Hassett—and there encircling the name was her ring. At least, it was on the northwest corner of the book as it lay on the shelf. Was the ring, she asked me, apported to that place? Would the name Fitzgerald have meaning if she knew the ring's entire history? At any rate her dream had imparted information.

Akin to the dream state is, of course, the trance. Here my own experience numbers thousands of instances and I suppose I know of a hundred or more persons whose trance mediumship offers veridical material. Sometimes the trance knowledge is disclosed through automatic writing. I am sure I must know a thousand persons who "do automatic writing," in trance or out. Sometimes the ability so to write comes upon an individual rather suddenly in the form of an almost uncontrollable urge to sit down and write, but more often it is the second stage of psychic development following use of a ouija board. Sometimes it has to be cultivated.

For instance, Dexter C. Buell, director of The Railway Educational Bureau of Omaha, Nebraska, set himself to develop the gift after he had met a physician in New England whose automatic writing appeared reliable. Buell sat at his desk on a regular schedule for a short time each day for a number of weeks before his pencil showed any inclination toward more than a few general Spencerian scrawls; then vague letters began to appear; some words;

and at last messages from a son who had died when 21 years old. The sum of the writings over several years is a body of consistent, intelligent and highly interesting material about the nature of the after-life.

Some automatic writing appears to be a mixture of the contents of the subconscious with information which the mind of the subject could not normally have available, and some is of a high order of dependability whether accepted as dictated by an outside intelligence or as the discernment of the freed mind of the subject.

Paranormal action differs from paranormal cognition in being observable to the eyes or ears of everyone in a room. Ordinarily the movement of objects in a characteristic manner depends upon muscular action on the part of someone. Books do not walk around the room, nor do coins toss themselves. However, I have seen objects moved about without an agent, and watched levitation.

Poltergeistic effects are a different matter. The knockings, rappings, senseless movement of seen and unseen objects and the like have been experienced by many persons whose word I cannot doubt, as well as by personalities in history whose word I also cannot doubt.

Anyone who has read the many volumes of the Wesley journals and letters is familiar with the poltergeistic interference, almost amounting at times to persecution, which the family experienced. At first the psychic disturbances at Epworth Vicarage, where the Rev. Samuel Wesley was rector of the church in 1716, were attributed to trickery, then to the devil. But the mother of John Wesley disagreed with these explanations. She had had a brother, in service with the East India Company, who had disappeared and never been heard of again, and she and her seven daughters took it for granted that these phenomena were connected with this brother, whom they called Old Jeffrey.

On January 12, 1717, the mother of John Wesley wrote:

"One night it made such a noise in the room over our heads as if several people were talking; then ran up and down stairs, and was so outrageous that we thought the children would be frightened, so your father and I rose and went down in the dark to light a candle. Just as we came to the bottom of the broad stairs, having hold of each other, at my side there seemed as if somebody had emptied a bag of money at my feet, and on his side as if all the bottles under the stairs (which were many) had been dashed into a thousand pieces. We passed through the hall into the kitchen and got a candle and went to see the children. The next night your father got Mr. Hoole to lie at our house and we all sat together till one or two o'clock in the morning and heard the knocking as usual. Sometimes it would make a noise like the winding up of a jack; and other times, as that night Mr. Hoole was with us, like a carpenter planing deals; but most commonly it knocked three and stopped and then thrice again and so many hours together."

Hetty Wesley reports that she heard "something like a man in a loose nightgown trailing after him" coming down the stairs behind her. The noises answered knock for knock and came in any part of the house. At family prayers at the names of King George and the Prince, the knocks became very agitated. Rev. Samuel Wesley tried to speak to them but the only answer he received was "two or three feeble squeaks a little louder than the chirpings of a bird, but not like the voice of rats which I have often heard." Nancy Wesley was once lifted up with the bed in which she sat. She jumped off the bed and said that surely Old Jeffrey would not run away with her. Fearfully she sat on the bed again whereupon the bed was lifted several times to a considerable height. The Wesleys had a mastiff dog who always whimpered in terror when these things happened and snuggled close to the people in the house.

The letters and published narrative of Susannah, Emilia and Molly Wesley contain these comments:

"We heard a great noise as if a piece of sounding metal was thrown down outside our chamber. It would answer to my mother if she stamped on the floor and bid it. . . . It was more loud and fierce if anyone said it was rats or due to natural causes. . . . The sounds very often seemed in the air in the middle of the room. . . . It never came by day until mother had ordered the horn blown. [This refers to a horn which Mrs. Wesley had ordered blown in all the rooms with the idea of scaring away any intruding entity.] . . . After that time scarce anyone could go from one room to another without the latch being lifted up before they touched it. . . . Whether the clock went right or wrong it always came as near as could be guessed about a quarter to ten in the night. . . . The room trembled as it passed along, and the doors shook exceedingly, so that the clattering of the latches was very loud. . . . The children were asleep, but panting, trembling, and sweating exceedingly. . . . My father adjured it, but it seemed to take no notice, at which he became angry and called it a deaf and dumb devil and again adjured it to speak. When he had done it knocked on the bed's head so loudly as if it would break it to shivers. . . . The Rev. Mr. Hoole (Vicar of Haxey) read prayers once, but it knocked as usual at the prayers for the king."

Once one begins to keep track of reports of poltergeistic phenomena, they seem less rare than might be supposed but the worth of the record depends upon the veracity, training and general character of the reporter.[1]

[1] As this book reaches the proof stage newspapers are featuring accounts of poltergeist phenomena involving a family in suburban Long Island, New York.

Among the varieties of psychophysical interaction, one of the commonest is billet reading in which the sensitive holds in his hand a sealed letter or a folded paper and discloses the contents without, of course, looking at what is written. My object reading is more likely to be accurate when I am in trance. For instance, not long ago a woman came to me after a meeting and held out an unusual ring which she asked me to psychometrize. Frankly, I was not in the mood and I suggested that she bring it to me at the next meeting. This she did, but she waited until I was in trance to present it. Fletcher announced patly that the woman who originally owned the ring had had her head cut off. Later the present owner told me something of the ring's history; it had once belonged to Mary, Queen of Scots.

Olga Worrall of Baltimore is good at psychometry. One day a friend of mine handed one of her pearl earrings to Olga and asked her what she got from it. At once Olga hunched over so that she seemed smaller and somewhat stooped and began to talk a rapid gibberish with many high accented syllables. Olga said, "The woman who gave you this earring is small and talks a language I don't know. She lives on the other side of the world, as far away as you can get and not be starting back here again. She has wealth but she is surrounded by poor people to whom her heart goes out so that she is always dividing with them. She has suffered a great deal, some of it because of war, I think. She gave you these earrings with real love and gratitude." My friend then explained that the earrings were given her by a small Chinese woman in Macassar, on the Island of Celebes. My friend knows Chinese and had often talked with her Chinese friend. The Chinese woman lives on her estate but during the Japanese occupation, when so many of the male members of her own family were killed, many poor people also lost everything they owned, so she allowed them to build huts on her property.

The fact that Olga Worrall also has diagnostic clairvoyance, as well as being able to discern and describe discarnates who may be in the room, supports the theory that an individual who develops clairvoyance in one direction can with training turn it in many directions.

Probably no other psychic phenomenon has been the subject of more fireside tales or produced more shivers up the spine than the subject of apparitions and hauntings. This is also a subject which has received a great deal of critical attention. In 1886 the Society for Psychical Research in Britain published the results of a twelve-year systematic inquiry into the reality of phantasmal appearances made by a committee of careful investigators who interviewed nearly six thousand persons who claimed to have seen ghosts. Their report was cautiously summarized: "Between death and apparitions a connection exists not due to chance alone. This we hold a proved fact." Other studies have been made on the Continent and in America. Currently Dr. Hornell Hart, formerly of Duke University, is collecting examples of phantasms of both the dead and the living.

Many persons do not realize that phantasms of the living are more common, perhaps twice over, than those of the dead, and that some excellent work has been done experimentally in producing apparitions; that is, a person may concentrate upon appearing to a certain individual in another location and cause himself to "appear" to the subject he has chosen.

Commonly the apparition of a restless earth-bound discarnate who continues to haunt the scene of his own death or his own habitat, attempting to convey a message about the method of his demise, is called a ghost. But everybody knows that a ghost is or isn't!

Ghosts have played their part in history and so have specters—who are usually considered imaginary apparitions as contrasted with the real thing. Plutarch records of Brutus: "A little before he left Asia he was sitting alone in his tent, in a dim light at a late hour. The whole army lay in sleep and silence, while the general, wrapped in meditation, thought he perceived something enter his tent; turning towards the door he saw a horrible and monstrous spectre standing silently by his side. 'What art thou?' said he boldly. 'Art thou god or man, and what is thy business with me?' The spectre answered, 'I am thy evil genius, Brutus! Thou wilt see me at Philippi.' To which Brutus calmly replied, 'I'll meet thee there.' When the apparition was gone he called to his servants, who told him they had neither heard any voice, nor seen any vision."

What is seen to be an apparition is a question that puzzles investigators. In a sitting with D. D. Home, one of the foremost mediums of modern times, a man of intelligent curiosity once asked Home's control how apparitions make themselves visible. The answer was, "At times we make passes over the individual to cause him to see us; sometimes we make the actual resemblance of our former clothing appear exactly as we were known to you on earth; sometimes we project an image that you see; sometimes you see us as we are with a cloudlike aura of light around us." If I could change the phrase "make passes over the individual" to "augment the field of energy around an individual," and change, "make the actual resemblance" to "mold ectoplasm into the semblance" then I should say that I have seen all these methods of manifestation.

Moreover, I once had encounter with a ghost myself, and in an English country house, just where the encounter should take place. I was spending a weekend with an amusing old lady, Lady Elizabeth Mosley, who told me that she had put me in her haunted room because of course I was one person who was not afraid of ghosts, hobnobbing with them daily as I did. The room she gave me was enormous; it was also cold. When I climbed into the huge poster bed I pulled an eider-down comforter over me, and I also left the door open a bit to admit some of the warmer air of the hall. That end of the hall was not lighted; what need had a ghost of light? I had fallen into a sound sleep when suddenly I felt the comforter being pulled from my shoulders. I could see no one beside the bed but definitely a hand had clutched that bedcover. I held the comforter in place as best I could but the Thing tugged harder and finally the cover was actually pulled out of my hands and floated out the door and trailed down the hall. After a very restless night I went down to breakfast at a late hour. As I came into the room, a fellow guest, an irascible and determined gentleman, was telling about returning from a meeting the previous evening at a very late hour indeed to find his bed with too few blankets and himself chilled to the marrow. So he had stealthily made his way down the dark corridor to the old haunted room and pulled an eider-down quilt off the unused bed. So then I told him that he had also pulled ten years off my life in the process.

The subject of apports stirs as much controversy as any other psychic interest—an apport being an object materialized before the eye. I have heard people tell about having valuable objects appear for them in a time of need. One woman—an estimable woman, too—insists that time and again she has had coins appear on her floor or in her hatbox when she desperately needed money for some needy person. This money, she says, always bears the date of some coin which has been declared lost by the government, for she has checked up on some of these silver dollars and gold pieces. I was as skeptical as the next one about such fortuitous fortune until I myself had a peculiar experience in England back in the late twenties.

A small group of us met at the home of Catherine Barkel. There were Sir Arthur Conan Doyle and Lady Doyle, Hannen Swaffer and his wife, Mrs. Stobart, Francis Fast and myself. Catherine Barkel was herself the medium and we sat on the lawn in broad daylight. She went quickly into trance and one of the group held her by the wrist. Soon her Indian guide took over and said the "little people" had brought certain objects of value which had been lost on ships sunk at sea or in other ways. At once in Mrs. Barkel's free hand, lying open in her lap, appeared a precious stone for each of us. The next day Doyle took them to a jeweler who appraised them at several hundred pounds. There was no fraud. Mrs. Stobart had her diamond set in a locket which she wore as long as I knew her. The others received an amethyst, emerald or ruby, and mine was an old-fashioned garnet which I later had set also.

I have seen Swaffer's collection of old silver spoons which were dropped into the middle of the floor of his drawing room in the same manner. On one occasion when Mrs. Swaffer wanted them initialed—they were all plain spoons of a simple design—a cork, marked with an S, floated down. To be sure, such things could not happen in a world governed by the laws we now apprehend, but they did happen.

Certainly among psychic manifestations would have to be included some of the performances of hatha-yoga. Certain yogins will run barbed hooks through their wrists, hang braziers of burning coals on them, carry the coals for hours during a parade, then remove the sharp hooks from the wrists leaving no wound or scar and without any sign of the flesh's having been reddened by the heat of the coals. On my trip to New Zealand, I also saw Fiji fire-walkers. In an annual ceremony they walked across the forty-foot pit of red-hot coals and were not burned, although the heat arising from the pit held back the by-standers at thirty feet. To me it seemed obvious that they were hypnotized, but whether by the priest or in a state of self-induced trance, I did not know.

When Dr. Walter F. Prince directed the experimentation of the American Society for Psychical Research, he had certain physiological tests made on me while I was in trance. The customary knee-joint reaction was absent which disturbed one of the medical men present. He said a subject might have the same reaction if he had syphilis, so I had to take a Wassermann and repeat the performance before he concluded that the trance state itself inhibited certain customary nervous reactions.

Nonmedical healing, known as spiritual healing, is a form of psychophysical interaction governed by laws we no more understand, as yet, than we comprehend the methods of producing apports. A force apparently operates on living matter to effect a change—but what force and why only on certain persons? Astute men are hunting answers. A friend of mine saw Julius Weinberger of the research staff of Radio Corporation of America attempt to detect a so-called healing force which seems to emanate from the hands of Ambrose Worrall, consulting engineer with Martin Aircraft Company, Baltimore, and from Dr. Michael Ash, of London. Since experiments on this force are still under way, I do not quote the tentative findings, but in some persons at some times there is a current strong enough to deflect a magnetic needle. One theory has been advanced that certain healers act as the positive pole over against the patient who acts as a negative pole in the exchange of energy, and vice versa; thus healers whose force is positive may have great success with certain patients and none with others. Others who are studying the matter feel that this theory is relevant but over-simplified. They agree that each cell in the body is an electric battery but also each cell, they hold, utilizes a vital energy, magnetic in kind, known to Eastern peoples as prahna, a force more manipulable than electricity, more readily drawn in from the universe itself. It is primarily this force, they feel, which the healer can direct to the needy organ or through the pituitary gland to the individual as a whole. Moreover, a patient can draw in this force without the aid of a healer if he realizes the fact.

This is a field in which much more study is needed. With the current stress laid by medicine upon the psychosomatic elements in healing, more physicians feel justified in being open-minded, even in experimenting in this field. Witness to this fact are the five seminars on spiritual healing which have been held at Wainwright House in Rye, New York, all of which were attended by distinguished medical men and women as well as by persons working directly in the field of spiritual healing. To date, too many non-medical healers have over-claimed and resented medical examination of their patients, and at the same time too many medical men have refused to acknowledge non-medical healing even when it is as apparent as any ever produced by medicine or surgery.

I know many persons doing effective spiritual healing, some through the orthodox channel of the laying on of hands, the use of holy oil, a special blessing with the partaking of the Eucharist; some through a simple formula devised by the healer himself; some—as with Ambrose Worrall—without any formula, ceremony or theory. People are cured; the disease with which they were afflicted before the healing does not return. Plenty of case studies are available, and although most are inadequately documented, some—such as those kept by Dr. Leslie Weatherhead's staff of healers at City Temple in London—have meticulously recorded medical histories.

In 1945 I was in Fort Lauderdale, Florida, scheduled to lecture to a large audience when I came down with a severe case of laryngitis. On the night of the lecture I felt much too sick to appear on a platform, and besides my voice was only a squeak. Those in charge of the meeting were overwhelmed for they knew many people were driving some distance to attend the lecture; if I could only do the open clairvoyance, even a small amount, then the audience would know that every attempt had been made. Finally I acquiesced in appearing if only to prove I could not speak. A substitute lecturer was engaged.

When I arrived for the meeting a stranger came backstage and asked if I would allow a spiritual healer, Clinton Stone, to heal me. Obviously I would be delighted to be healed, but I felt the time a bit short and the case a mite stubborn. The stranger brought Mr. Stone into the room—a quiet man with an air of serenity and spiritual calm. He greeted me with assurance, asked no questions, put his hand on my throat and told me to relax. And as he spoke I felt my throat relax, and then tingle with vitality. Mr. Stone said, "Dr. Stearns says it is all right now." And it was all right. I went onto the platform, spoke easily for forty-five minutes, followed by a half hour of clairvoyance.

Since then I have taken, and sent, a good many persons to Clinton Stone. Many have been healed completely and I have a file of their testimonials; all have been helped. The partnership, Stone and Stearns—Stearns being the discarnate member—is effective.

The feeling of vitality which I felt under Mr. Stone's

hands seems one mark of this kind of healing. Many have told me that after Ambrose Worrall has given them a treatment they feel the same reaction. Often with Worrall one treatment produces spectacular change; at other times the healing requires a series of treatments. Sometimes no healing takes place. Worrall attests that age, sex, severity of the disease make no difference, nor does the presence or lack of a feeling of empathy, but at the same time there are persons for whom he knows at once he can do nothing; not the particularly or hopelessly ill, either, but just "certain persons." He has no theory to advance but a good many recorded facts and hopes from them eventually to adduce a tentative theory.

In the whole psychic field popular credence does not wait on facts but rather upon an acceptable supportive hypothesis as to the nature of man and matter.

If all these hints, nudges and conclusions mediated by discarnate friends are in the right direction, then latently everyone is psychic. This is a fact I had been suspecting for years.

CHAPTER 17

Expansion of Consciousness

IT TAKES only one instance to prove that consciousness operates free of the body. For scientific observation one instance may be of interest, but for practical purposes expanded consciousness needs to be reproducible, reliable, and amenable to direction.

It is my experience that expansion of consciousness can be developed. In other words, that psychic faculties can be induced and trained. My spasmodic psychic faculties were trained. I have wakened and trained others. Perhaps disciplined is a better word. Moreover, there are rules for this discipline. Some of them I stumbled upon, although they have been known for thousands of years; some were taught to me. There is nothing original about them. They are the laws which operate any time, any place. They may be phrased variously to suit different cultures but however stated they produce results when followed.

It is important that consciousness should be expanded. The race needs to live in the larger context of understanding which psychic faculties permit. Moreover, I suspect that an individual can only reach full maturity when his consciousness is expanded. A man with psychic gifts, if his faculties are reliable and if he is free of self-interest, can help his fellows in ways no other can help. Obligation is constantly laid upon young people to get into the service fields, such as medicine, the ministry, social science and the like. After a lifetime of observation of the needs of men, I believe that young people should also get into this field; especially educated young people who know what discipline means in other fields and who bring their training to bear upon their new endeavor.

There are a few prerequisites.

Anyone who wants to train for psychic development has to approach his task with an unclouded ego. Other service fields have their Hippocratic oath, their pledges, their subscribed unselfishness, but men can succeed professionally and by-pass their pledges. In this field deviation from the goal spells ultimate defeat. To be sure, selfish persons can make progress but only to a certain level and they run grave risks. Soul knowledge is meant for those concerned with souls. If knowledge not used is sin, so, too, is the acquiring of insight for other than its intrinsic purposes.

Anyone who wants to train psychically has to be capable of sustained endeavor. Spasmodic efforts are worse than none.

An open mind is also important but an open nature is more important; this is the clarity the saints speak of and the scientist knows, at least in relationship to his work. One needs to line up at the beginning with truth in action, speech and attitude. A lie detector registers untruth because the psychophysical mechanism registers deviation but a student does not always know, consciously, when he has departed from the truth. In any walk of life the ability to discern truth is rare, and the ability to speak the truth even more rare. In psychic work this careful handling of truth is a necessity if one ever expects to have open vision.

Working with a teacher is a tremendous aid. There are corrections to be made in working habits and also within the student himself, which a teacher will point out. Correction is a delicate matter but also a stern matter. Another great usefulness of a teacher is his ability to sense when a student is pushing himself, trying to go too fast and hence delaying progress. Primarily, however, a teacher is a way-shower, and a student who keeps his eye on him will find encouragement in subtle ways. Of course it is possible to train without a teacher. Someone must have done it in the first place!

Now I realize these were some of the points Swami Yogananda was trying to get across to me and now I know that I would have gone further, faster, and saved myself enormous suffering if I had taken in what he meant. So now I try to get the same points over to my students— occasionally with success.

Psychic development has to progress on three levels at once—body, emotion, mind. The three components cannot be separated but they must be worked at independently. None of the three dares lag or the other two cannot proceed.

First at the body level. I now believe that body discipline is the most difficult if one includes all of the body appetites. In this lifetime and for sound reasons the training of the body is a part of expanding consciousness. The body has to be made fit to support the developing mind and the refined emotions; if it is not made fit then the whole project falls short by the degree of the body's unfitness. A fat person may become psychic but he would be a better psychic if he trimmed down; an emaciated person may become psychic but he would sustain his effort better if he were well nourished. A tense person, however, is under the greatest handicap of all. I never met a tense person who was a dependable psychic.

Every student who wants to develop psychically has to learn to relax.

Requirements for this type of relaxation are two: the student must be comfortable; he must have his spine straight. Often the two requirements seem impossible of fulfillment at the same time. If the spine is unaccustomed to being straight, then to insist that it remain straight is to put unused muscles under tension and to become uncomfortable, hence tense. If this is the student's predicament, he would do well to postpone his next step until he gets his spine in better line. However, he can begin before he has perfect posture. Ideally at the beginning of each session an individual will spend some time in limbering up and stretching until he senses the body as a porous thing made up of atoms which are immeasurably far apart and free in space. The body is not solid; its matter is not compressed. Its openness has to be felt kinesthetically before it is as pliable as it needs to be. When a student senses his own pliability and can be comfortable while maintaining a straight spine, then it does not matter too much whether he is lying down, sitting, or standing up.

Relaxation has, ultimately, to be complete. It has to extend from the tips of the toes to the hair follicles atop the head, but neither is the best place to begin to relax. The eyes are probably the first consideration. One who can relax his eyes can relax. Let them feel loose; let the lids droop until they seem heavy, without response. The eyes themselves move easily on the eyeball, like leaves gently skimming the surface of a pond; then they cease to move; why should they move? They are relaxed. The nose is relaxed; the restless inquisitive nose is taking itself a rest. The mouth has no further response; it is closed, lightly, and content to stay closed forever. The cheeks are relaxed which means the ears also; the ears feel as large and as limp as the ears of a sleeping spaniel; they droop; they lie softly against the neck. All the features let go lazily. The forehead is no longer wrinkled; how could it be with the ears relaxed? The scalp is too large for the cranium, as an attempt to wrinkle it would prove, but it is too relaxed to wrinkle.

After the head, the neck and shoulders. The stiff self-willed shoulders! The shoulders which have carried so many burdens not theirs to carry; the shoulders which have edged and butted their way through so many crowds and jams! Now they are too relaxed to remember. The muscles which hold the breastbone back and the wing-bones out and the arms in place—all of them are relaxed.

Then the feet. Way off down there, the feet. The tense cramped small toe, the half-forgotten middle toes; they come to life in letting go. Each side of the foot; both feet. Each leg, round about, inside and outside; the overworked knees; the underworked buttocks; all are relaxed. Then the trunk, muscle by muscle. This is the drowsy way to learn anatomy, by letting go, segment by segment.

In the process of learning to relax completely the student will discover the reason for the necessity of relaxation: a relaxed individual is detached. He does not feel bound to his body. He is aware of his body only distantly, with an unaccustomed sense of peace. His mind is not tethered by strain or pain. However, in being un-tethered the mind is not necessarily free for profitable pursuits because the disconcerting fact is that as a state of complete relaxation is reached the student, if alone, probably falls asleep.

A young person in our western world almost always needs sleep. For this business of psychic development he has to be awake, probably more acutely than he has ever been before, but he cannot be awake until he has caught up on his sleep; on the good deep relaxed sleep which he needs.

Perhaps for a week every time he tries to relax he will fall asleep. And then one day he will be discouraged by the fact that he always goes to sleep and so he will consider going to bed earlier, but the cultural drag upon him is very great. Like most of the people he knows, he stays out late, talks late, studies late, has a late snack, then, finally in sheer exhaustion winds the alarm clock and falls into bed. To undo the habits of years and to buck the current of custom takes more courage and more individuality than a student can usually muster. But the student who genuinely wants to expand his consciousness will take his habits in hand. He will develop some physiological curiosity and learn to play along with the laws of bodily well being. He might as well for his progress is limited if he neglects the body, or even slights it.

A day will come when the student is able to relax and stay awake. And then he sets himself to learning how to breathe.

And why, he is likely to ask, is special breathing so necessary? He gets along all right, he feels, on the kind of breathing he does habitually. The answer is that he will get along much better when he learns to breathe fully and rhythmically. Most untrained persons are shallow breathers; they utilize only a part of their lung capacity. Few know how to expand the diaphragm so that the abdomen is exercised; the advantages of the regular use of the abdominal muscles have to be experienced to be appreciated. Some teachers of breathing speak of low breathing, meaning the expansion of the lower diaphragm by the use of the abdominal muscles; of middle breathing, meaning the full expansion of the ribs; and of high breathing, meaning the filling of the upper lobes of the lungs so that the act of breathing is felt even under the collarbones. Attention may be directed to any one of these ways of breathing but the best way to breathe while training is to cultivate the full breath which encompasses them all. The full breath guarantees an adequate supply of oxygen to the system and this alone improves health and quickens the perceptions.

Not only does the breathing need to be full but it has to be gentle, even. The masters of breathing aver that when the breath is evenly controlled a feather held under the nose will not be stirred.

Full and even breathing needs also to be rhythmic. Rhythm is a psychological law. The beat of a healthy heart is rhythmic; the play of the muscles is rhythmic; the act of walking is rhythmic, as is the swing of the arms and slight turning of the body. Peristalsis is rhythmic; a good digestion is a rhythmic digestion. But rhythm is not more important to any of these processes than to breathing. A student who breathes rhythmically is in tune with himself; his organs are like orchestral instruments following the beat of the baton.

Teachers of breathing have developed many varieties of breath, some of them useful. There is a cleansing breath for which the student fills the lungs and forcibly expels the air through the mouth in a quick puff. There is the sustained breath in which a count of eight is made on inhaling, the breath held for four or eight counts, and then exhaled on eight counts. Sometimes the number is multiplied by two or even more.

While practice is the keynote of psychic expansion, discretion is surely the signature. A categorical don't applies to the more complicated forms of breathing which necessitate prolonged emptiness of the lungs. A teacher is necessary for advanced training and, as the ancients have it, "when the student is ready the teacher appears." This is not to say that advanced training is not important. The purest forms of concentration can only be maintained so long as the breath is held, and this feat may be learned.

It is not only how one breathes but what that matters. Air, of course; oxygen for the burning up of waste products in the blood. Fresh air, if possible; air which is uncontaminated by the waste products of our chimneys. In the atmosphere, we are told, there are trace elements, even cosmic rays, important to our well-being. But also air that is inhaled rhythmically, evenly, seems to contain something more than elements that can be chemically assayed; something extremely vitalizing. In the East it is called prahna.

Students of psychic development soon find out that rhythmic breathing has a peculiar effect in producing a peculiar kind of energy. What this energy is, is a debated question. Whatever its intrinsic nature, however, it is felt as a current, a definite force, a vitalizing agent. And it stimulates psychic development. Indeed, without it psychic development is impossible.

After the student has practiced rhythmic breathing for a time he will one day feel this ingathering of vitality, as if his body even in its most inert state were being animated. He senses it as a delicate centralizing force which seems to integrate the body and sharpen the faculties. His whole psychophysical organism has a feeling of expectancy, a sense of latent power.

This energy first seems to quicken the base of the spine, then rises up the course of the spine, sometimes lingering at certain points as a stream might pause to fill a pool before continuing its journey. If the spine is straight it will continue into the head and terminate behind the forehead in a faint pulsing sensation which seems to fill the cranium pleasantly. Sometimes there is then a quickening, or at least a definite awareness, of the solar plexus.

While the current is up the student will feel as if his whole being were at acute attention. He may hear a sound he has not heard before—a clear faint note; some describe it as the individual's keynote; some as the keynote of the universe. He may feel as if he were looking through an infinitely long telescope and seeing a tiny brilliant point of light, and he will know that the light has infinite significance. This is the time to visualize his own need, whatever it may be, and to lift it up, as if he were asking the universe to make plain the answer. He may get the answer in a flash of understanding or in a symbol or in a sentence. Or he may get instead a feeling of peace, assurance; if the latter, a more specific answer is likely to come to him in the ensuing hours or days. The experience will be short in time duration and then the vital current will fade out.

Sometimes at the next day's practice period the vital current will be felt only faintly; and the student may report, "Nothing much happened today." But if he goes on with his relaxation and breathing exercises he will soon find this vital energy coming in regularly, able to sustain concentration for increasing periods. Each day, he will go out from his practice period with a new vitality, as if he were connected with the magnetic currents of the universe.

Adepts of the East call this current *kundalini* and many books have been written about it. Westerners who have discovered it have done little in the way of documentation. This is a subject upon which much more work needs to be done by persons of our own culture. Here again a teacher is worth more than all the books, but without either book or teacher anyone who sets his mind to do so may find his own way. In fact, anyone who practices meditation is bound to stumble onto these basic facts.

In learning to relax, to breathe, and to pay attention to the energizing current, the wise student will not push himself. Short practice periods are more effective than longer periods in which attention cannot be sustained.

Also a faithful student will find himself altering many

of his daily habits. Just as he had to make up sleep before he could stay vividly awake, so he also finds that he needs to look to his physical nourishment. Heavy foods retard his breathing; too much food makes him resistant to the quickening current. Often an alert teacher talks about diet early in his course, but if he never mentions it, the alert student will discover that what he eats makes a difference. He will discover that alcohol and psychic development are incompatible, and I say this in face of the fact that I drank heavily for years while earning my living as a trance medium. He will also discover that tobacco clouds sensitivity. Of course, he may decide to smoke anyway, as I have done at times, but he is then saying that he wants only as much discipline as is comfortable. We all have to face up to the character implications of psychic training. Dodge them as we may, the tests come back and back until they are met. And then we take a seven-league stride.

Not only at the physical level will changes in the student's habits be necessary but at the emotional level. He will discover that if he is angry or even anxious he cannot breathe deeply, evenly and rhythmically. He has to choose between negative emotions and progress; he cannot have both. He will also discover that he cannot postpone meeting problems. When he first gets into training his problems may seem to become more acute. Basically, though, they are just one problem—coming to terms with himself and his circumstances. And this he will find himself doing with increasing ease and clarity as his training moves into the next phase—the discipline of the mind.

CHAPTER 18

Training in Expansion

WHEN HE HAS LEARNED to relax and breathe the student is ready to learn to concentrate. To a degree learning to relax and breathe has already taught him to concentrate for neither proper relaxation nor breathing can be accomplished without strict direction of attention. He is now ready to bring his mind to bear on things outside himself. In derivation the word "concentrate" means to bear center. He is ready to place some thing, some object, at the center of his attention and to hold his attention on the chosen object.

To begin this phase of his work, an harmonious place is an asset. In time he will be able to concentrate any place, any time, but in the beginning it pays to seek harmonious conditions without distractions. The student may want to use his office after hours when the typewriters are silent and the telephone has ceased to ring. Or it may be a bedroom, but one which is in order; or a quiet living room; or a corner of the kitchen. One good student, I recall, used to go into an empty church and there do her half-hour's concentration.

The next step is to choose an object and look at it. A pencil, a rose, a ring, a spoon, anything simple. If a student decides on a pencil, then let him really observe it. Let him note its length, thickness, shape, color; the way the eraser fits into the metal tip, the size of the tip, its indentations; the point, how it is sharpened, the exact shade of the lead. When he has observed that pencil carefully, he is ready to shut his eyes and try to recall every detail in sharp focus. One woman, at a time when she was in a hospital, tried this exercise on the light fixture above her bed; it was two weeks before she could recall every detail of that fixture, including the pattern of the shadow which the fixture cast upon itself and the ceiling.

After several practice periods on the characteristics of the pencil, the student is ready to concentrate on the pencil's meaning. What is a pencil good for? Does it fulfill its function? Here he may pause so intently that he finds himself inventing a better pencil! From what elements was the pencil derived? Where did the lead come from? What process brought it from beneath the earth's surface to its place in the pencil? Where did the wood originate? How did the tree look, where did it grow, when was it cut, what was its manufacturing process as it became a pencil?

Still with concentration, let imagination come into play. Let the student look at the room from the pencil's point of view. His hand becomes an enormous grasping mechanism; he himself is a giant. Other objects in the room— chairs, tables, lamps—take on different proportions. A cushioned davenport is a fearful thing; how easy to slip behind a cushion and be lost. The sharp teeth of a dog or a child are a threat. A pen is a rival, a book the product of its skill, a man an arbiter of fate.

Imagination gives way to empathy. Now empathy is a feeling quality. Absorbed in concentration the student begins to feel with the pencil until he encompasses it; it yields itself up to him. If the identity is sharp enough he may suddenly see or sense the person to whom the pencil formerly belonged. Or he may see an incident in which that pencil figured—the hasty signing of a deathbed will, a child's fright on his first day at school. Let him take note of the impression, but only in a relaxed, mildly curious fashion. This is not the time to question or analyze. After the period is over he may scrutinize his impressions. If they have to do with a person whom he knows, he may check up. But if the impression appears to have been misconstrued he must not be discouraged for he may have been more accurate than he thinks. Or he may have been wrong entirely. Or he may have no impression. Whatever the result, his next step is the same: choose another article and repeat the process. Observe, concentrate, identify. A day will come when he will pick up from some object information which could not have come through sensory channels. And this is the beginning of clairvoyance.

There is never a time to stop practicing relaxation, rhythmic breathing and concentration, just as there is never a time for a musician to quit practicing scales and arpeggios. But there is a time to go on to more complicated objects than a pencil. Someone's ring, perhaps, about which the student can check impression against fact; a letter sealed in its envelope; a hat whose owner is unidentified, but who can later authenticate impressions; a book in a plain cover; any object he can hold in his hands, see, feel, sense the weight and texture of. When he finds himself fairly regularly picking up knowledge from objects, he has become a psychometrist.

There are group techniques for work in psychometry. When a student finds himself beginning to be clairvoyant he is ready to join a group. Too early work with a group is usually a mistake unless the group is exceedingly carefully chosen and the teacher adept; and even so, the basic work of relaxation has to be done alone. A study group needs to be made up of alert, intelligent, sympathetic persons, of one mind about approaching their task with steadfast will, but at the same time they have to remain lighthearted about their undertaking. They have to be able to accept failure and delay debonairly but press right on.

In developing the technique of psychometry students may profitably co-operate on tests. Let someone prepare envelopes into which are put samples of simple substances such as sugar, salt, cream of tartar, pepper, cornstarch, flour and the like; pass the envelopes around the group and let each participant record what he thinks the envelopes contain. Or use opaque containers holding liquids such as water, milk, vinegar, salad oil, wine, orange juice, and so forth. Often, even at the first try, some student will have a definite taste sensation or will feel activity in the salivary glands. He may even sneeze over pepper. One class found the experiments with purgatives and emetics had harmless but embarrassing results.

Another group experiment is the exchange of articles for the purpose of sensing something of the article's history. A ring, a watch, a brooch, an earring, a special handkerchief, a business card, a letter, any article of which the owner more or less knows the history but with which the recipient has no familiarity. Let each student hold the article assigned him in his left hand and cup his right hand lightly over it; then close his eyes and register what is sensed or seen or felt or even heard. After six or eight minutes let the articles be returned to their owners and each student tell what he sensed or imagined. No impression should be held back, however trivial, for it may have meaning to the owner.

For instance, a girl in one class took from the man next to her a ring which he wore on his little finger; all she got was an impression of the color red, a beautiful bright red; nothing else. When she reported her impression the owner of the ring laughed, for the woman who had given him the ring wore a great deal of that particular shade of red and liked red objects in her house; he used to call her "Little Red." Another student, a man, who held a woman's watch could only report that instead of ticking, the watch "rang little bells, almost as if it was playing a tune"; he was embarrassed over what he felt to be his silly impression. But the owner of the watch played a xylophone and her best concert piece was one in which bells were imitated.

At first, in any class, there are likely to be a great many more misses than hits. Moreover, some persons seem constitutionally more adept than others. We say they are "sensitive" and the word applies both to their reaction to sensory impressions and to these extrasensory impressions. A sensitive person responds more readily to training, but few persons are accurate judges of their own sensitivity. A huge hulk of a fellow, always active and often boisterous, may prove to be not only "gentle with children and dogs" but sensitive to psychic training. On the other hand a thin, nervous woman who fancies herself sensitive may actually be so encased in self-interest that impressions of things and people around her never penetrate. These differences show up in psychic training.

Psychometrizing of persons is often done for the purpose of medical diagnosis. If the student feels led in this direction, then his first procedure is to run his hands lightly over the patient's body. Let him work with his eyes closed, centering attention through the perceptive process which is sometimes called the inner eye. As he touches the skin of the patient's face or arms he may feel a scratch or roughened spot with his tactile sense, but he may also sense bruises, congestion, inflammation or some other difficulty not discernible to the tactile sense. Let him note even the most fleeting impression; perhaps the patient will feel more opaque in the region of the chest, say, than in other parts of the body. Let him state what he feels. Even if the patient denies any trouble in the area of the chest, the student may be right. Or, of course, as a beginner he may be wrong. Either way, the important thing is to register and report his findings.

Let the student be alert to note various methods of response to the affected area. Do his hands feel cold over a certain area? Does he suddenly feel pain in his own body at a certain point and does that point correspond to the location of the pain in the patient? There is no right or wrong method of responding; each sensitive has to develop his own signals and interpret their meaning in his own way; the difficult part is to stay by the training when the signals are not yet clear, when the misses exceed the hits. Let him be consoled by one correct response. William James used to say that it takes only one white crow to prove that all crows are not black. Even so, it takes only one correct diagnosis which could not have come through sensory channels to prove that extrasensory diagnosis is possible.

Sometimes as a student is psychometrizing a patient he may feel an impulse to heal. He may sense a current flowing through his hands and be impressed to put his hand over the troubled area; or he may feel the healing current pulsing in his own forehead and be impressed to direct his attention to the patient as one might play a stream of water over a given area. Whatever form the urge to heal takes, this is the student's clue to follow. And his next step is to practice, practice, practice. Everyone he works on will not be healed, not even after he becomes proficient, but his responsibility is to become a reliable channel for the healing power, and this means training.

Some simple exercises may help to develop sensitivity

for diagnosis and healing. Let the student sit relaxed before a mirror in a dimly lighted room and see if he can perceive any sort of emanation coming from the reflected image. Some see an outflowing like a delicate mist; a reflection of an emanation from the student's body. Once it is sensed the student may then see it coming from other people, and when an individual is ill this emanation is likely to appear thinner, or to seem to have holes in it, or to flow in a jerky fashion. The student begins to interpret what he sees in terms of the patient's condition.

Let the student hold his right hand above a mirror and then his left. Ascertain whether one hand is slightly cooler than the other. The warmer hand is usually interpreted as being the positive aspect of the vital current and should be placed over the affected portion of the body with the left hand beneath the body, the theory being that a current passes between the two. Undoubtedly the current is too fine to be picked up by any instrument known at present—although good scientists are working on just this thing—but "it acts like a current."

Let one student close his eyes while another student moves his hands slowly, at a distance of about three inches, over and around the head and shoulders of the percipient who tries to sense whether the passes are made upward or downward. Most students feel the downward passes as positive; that is, they make the body feel relaxed, in line, and often relieve tension and, with it, pain. Let each student in the group act as recipient while each of the others tries the motion of the hands—often called magnetic passes in the old literature. Usually one student will set up a more marked current than the others and usually he proves to be the one who is interested, or becomes skilled, in healing.

Let the student seat himself comfortably so that he can

breathe rhythmically, then let him close his eyes and place one hand on each knee, bringing the thumb and forefinger of each hand together until they touch. This position is sometimes called "locking vibrations." Then let him direct his inner gaze to the bridge of the nose. If the body remains quiet and the gaze stedfast, he will find that concerns of the day will fade away and in this state he is likely to receive some definite clairvoyant impressions.

Both psychometry and clairvoyance are forms of clairsentience—clear knowing—and one is likely to induce the other. Sometimes a student while psychometrizing will have a clairvoyant experience; for instance, he may see an incident in the patient's past which accounts, at least in part, for the present illness. Or he may see a discarnate who is helping him to help the patient. Or he may see a living person who is in some way tied into the problem which has produced the illness.

A student who has developed his psychic faculties to the point where he can glimpse data which could not be acquired by normal means may find the information coming to him through symbols. Some symbols seem to be generally accepted, at least in our culture. All the sensitives I know who see symbols would accept a dove as meaning peace, for instance, or a cross as indicating suffering. At the same time some students develop their own individual interpretations. For instance, one student reported that whenever he saw a blue star he knew a message was coming to him personally.

Akin to the symbols seen clairvoyantly are the symbols thrown up by dreams. Most dreams are, indeed, symbols of problems confronting the dreamer. A student can train his mind in sleep to produce dreams whose meaning he will not mistake. The technique for training is to lie down comfortably and relax completely, then inform the deep mind specifically as to the problem, instructing it to bring to consciousness whatever may be presented in a dream. When he wakens, whether in the night or the next morning, let the student jot down every fragment of any dream he can remember. After a short time of faithful practice he will find himself "dreaming sense."

It is not unusual for a student in a class in psychic development to fall spontaneously into trance. Now a trance is a sleeplike state in which the faculties are released from their usual sensory limitations. There are physiological marks of a trance which differentiate it from ordinary sleep, primarily the slower tempo of the autonomic nervous system and lack of the usual response to pain. The person in trance is only called a medium if in his trance he acts as a go-between for incarnate and discarnate entities. It is possible to fall into trance and merely dream clairvoyantly, or to walk somnambulistically. No matter what goes on in trance the individual usually wakens with the feeling of having been asleep. He has no sense of time.

In training to learn how to go into trance a hypnotist is often helpful. He may be the teacher. The technique of inducing a hypnotic state is well documented in medical literature. Once the student has lost touch with his objective surroundings, then the hypnotist may proceed to give him directions. If he is training for mediumship, the instruction will probably be to look about him and report whomever he sees. If he reports on other living persons in the room the hypnotist accepts his report and at the proper time terminates that day's session. There needs to be a feeling of mutual confidence between the hypnotist and the student and this may require several sessions.

In the next lesson the hypnotist may ask the student, after he is hypnotized, to look about the room and report on other persons who have lived in the same room. The student may or may not be able thus to go back in time, but if the hypnotist is patient and commendatory most students can thus extend their awareness. The hypnotist may also ask the student to go back into his own past and tell what he was doing on his fifteenth birthday, say, or on his second birthday; to describe his presents, his party, his relatives, the decorations in his room. Some students find no difficulty in this kind of regression.

After a few sessions the hypnotist may then suggest that there are other presences in the room; individuals who have left this earth but are as much alive as ever. He asks the student to describe anyone he sees. Perhaps the student sees no such person and begins instead to describe some other living individual who once lived there. But if the instructor is patient the student may come back to the initial instruction and offer the information that now there is someone present. His grandfather has just come in. The hypnotist may ask for a description of the grandfather, and as the two, hypnotist and student, discuss the third party, the hypnotist may explain that while this is indeed the subject's grandfather, the grandfather has been dead for quite some time. No doubt he has something to say, some message he would like to send to another member of the family.

Often the answers of the hypnotized student will be very slow as if he were trying to read a message which is thrown on a screen letter by letter. Actually, he is trying to translate thought impressions or symbols into words. The hypnotist can only encourage and wait. After a few sessions the subject will become more proficient. The hypnotist will probably instruct him to proceed with confidence; just to say whatever he thinks he is hearing; and not to linger too long with one personality but to turn to the next who may be waiting his turn.

Thus in a series of sessions the student learns the techniques for making contact with discarnate personalities and bringing back in words what they are trying to impart.

But it is not always convenient to have a hypnotist at hand. Sooner or later the student will wish to put himself into trance. Let him lie quietly in a relaxed state, aware that he is in command of the situation and that the inner censor who never sleeps will allow no harm to come to him. A pleasant sense of expectancy colors his passivity. Let him breathe regularly but not too deeply as he instructs his mind to report back whatever it sees or hears while he sleeps. If he has been hypnotized previously he may recall the hypnotist's voice giving him instructions. If he has never been hypnotized he may find it helpful to gaze at a bright light until his vision blurs. Whatever thoughts come to mind, let them pass on lazily like clouds in a summer sky. Soon they will tend to blur and he will fall asleep.

As the student lets go of consciousness the body may tend to jerk, as it often does in falling into normal sleep. Sometimes it may contort a bit, just as a sleeping body may at times thrash around briefly. Then the body will be at peace. As the trance deepens the student may at times gesture and show some animation, as does a person talking in his sleep.

Once he is in trance he will usually begin of his own accord to describe whatever and whomever he sees and to voice their communication. A variety of personalities may come, some of them returning again and again in subsequent trance sessions. But one day—it may be the first occasion or it may be after many sessions—some discarnate will identify himself and say that he is to be a permanent control; henceforth he will act as the director of operations on the discarnate side.

When the medium gets to know this personality so that

he visualizes him as well as senses his presence, he may find it helpful when he wishes to go into trance simply to recall the face of his control. If he knew the control in life it is easier to visualize him with characteristic expression and mannerisms. As the student lies quietly, beginning to feel drowsy, visualizing this face, he will probably see it more clearly on the in-breath, as if the face came toward him; then it will fade a bit as the student exhales, swinging back and forth with the breath until he feels the other face and his own become one.

Once a control has signified that the relationship is permanent, the medium will find it much easier to slip into trance. He develops a feeling that the control is ready and dependable. Since a control has to be a discarnate whose overall energy pattern is harmonious with the energy pattern of the medium and since each individual is a composite of energies embodying his emotional, intellectual and spiritual attainments, the medium may be sure that he will not be taken over by a discarnate whose nature is greatly different from his own. In other words, a medium whose intention is honest will find himself working with a control of like intention.

When a medium of modest intellectual capacity purports to have a control who was an intellectual giant on this earth, it is time to question whether or not either the medium or the control is masquerading. Or if a medium of dubious reputation claims a control who gives the name of one of the saints, it is also time to question a hoax—especially if the "saint" issues orders which no high-minded living individual would issue. Indeed, any control who issues orders and attempts to substitute for the free will of the sitters, or who tries to direct the minutiae of their lives, should be suspected of pretending to be other than he is.

There is nothing sacrosanct about a medium or a control and both should be expected to pass whatever test of authenticity seems reasonable. Identification is difficult even in this life, as anyone can demonstrate who asks his best friend at the other end of a telephone line to give positive proof that he is who he says he is.

While for some students psychic development is a steady growth, for others it is a time of trial, even of tragedy. A student may begin to do automatic writing in which a benevolent source seems to be giving sound advice, and then the advice becomes malicious or ridiculous. The discarnate communicator may instruct the student to perform futile and difficult tasks "as a test." But one thing is sure: a malevolent entity can gain access to the student's mind only through some weakness of character—pride, desire for fame or power, overwillingness to set aside judgment or to avoid making choices, antagonisms, hate. The pure in heart are safe and those truly devoid of self-interest find unseen collaborators of the same sort.

In every phase of psychic endeavor there are laws at work and the adept quite as much as the student has to keep lining himself up with them. Physical fitness, moral responsibility, mental equilibrium, emotional harmony, spiritual expectancy, a dedicated will—all of these are the supportive concomitants of expanded awareness.

CHAPTER 19

The Pathway of Prayer

As I BECAME increasingly interested in helping other people develop their psychic faculties it occurred to me that I had never known a group which met regularly for prayer but that someone in the group, and often several, developed psychic ability. Then I realized that I had never known an individual who prayed insistently to find the will of God for his life who did not develop some measure of extrasensory awareness. He might not call it that, but he had it.

At first I asked myself why this should be true, but after I joined the healing group which brought me out of alcoholism I began to get clues. Once I got inside the group I saw that each person there was trying to get in touch with God. Unabashed, he wanted God to make him over. He wanted to become the kind of person God intended him to be—and this he felt would be his real self. So he was always listening inwardly. He was expecting to be informed. He would speak of trying to be open to leading and this is a condition of keen and quiet anticipation.

I could see that people in this healing group were becoming bigger persons. I could see their minds take on a reach they never had before. They began to understand

people around them. Many of them reported that when
"something" told them to do so-and-so and they followed
the nudge they would find themselves in some place where
they were needed at exactly that time. Astounding stories
of arriving just where someone was desperate for help.
Sometimes I would hear the remark "I seemed to hear
something say . . . ," or "His face flashed before me
and . . . ," or "I heard her call my name so I went to the
telephone and . . ." At the meetings no one talked about
clairaudience or telepathy but they told their experiences.
Obviously no one was working for psychic gifts; the gifts
were just coming along as needed.

This fact that many post-alcoholics have psychic experience has been noticed by so many post-alcoholics themselves that one of them is accumulating data to make a
serious study. It seemed plain that more than coincidence
was at work. He decided the thing at work was an organiz-
ing factor which struggles to assert itself in all nature; the
impetus which causes the tree, the stone, the crystal to make
itself whole when injured, the inner wisdom which enables
the human body to maintain a measure of health against
great odds. This is the God-force emancipating every
creature from its bounds until it reaches its own implicit
perfection. At the level of human personality we have to
will that this God-force have its perfect way.

With this in the back of my mind it occurred to me one
day that every individual who prayed consistently was
doing the same thing—offering himself to God's purposes,
getting stripped down and then built up, and finding that
the building up included an extension of awareness. This
was the reason that so many people in prayer groups tended
to develop psychic faculties.

Personally I had not always prayed this kind of prayer.
Like the Prodigal Son before he came to himself, I prayed

"give me" instead of "make me." In those days I did not want to be made over after some pattern God might have in mind; I just wanted him to work along with me in improving my condition. This is the conventional pattern most of us follow until we are desperate.

The process of prayer is the process of being made over. This is not a thing that can be done in spurts. There has to be a definite and regular time for two-way exchange of thought. It is because consistency is so difficult that the transformation takes so long. Day by day, however, we are revealed to ourself in proportion to the attention we give the matter, not only in terms of our failure but also in terms of our unlimited possibilities. And as we begin to sense our real self we are sure to see our actions in a new light. Hence we may suddenly realize that we have to change our way of earning a livelihood, or that we have to shift our economic standards and modify our social pattern, or change our friends and our pleasures. Oddly few of the changes seem like losses because the satisfaction of becoming ourself is very great. And the comfort of knowing we are moving in line with God's intention is even greater. Actually the two are inseparable and both are a part of the answer to our prayer.

Even though we know that God knows our problems, including the way we came to be tangled into them, still we usually feel that we have specifically to get them out before him. Some people talk them out just as they would to a friend. They may speak aloud or they may whisper as if the least expression were enough for his ear. Some explain their dilemma mentally. However the problem is presented the prayer is the same—"God help me!"

This call for help is the key to answered prayer because we would not be holding up our problem to God, and ourself with it, unless we had some belief that he could help us. The strength of our belief is the measure of the answer we will receive. According to our faith, so shall it be! This is *the* fundamental law of prayer. Everyone who has spoken with authority on prayer has told us this thing. It was the keynote of the teaching of Jesus. Believe that you have it, and you have it. Faith is the activating agent. The answer to our need is available but it cannot get in to us until we call for it and believe it will come. I wish I knew how to make this point clear for it is paramount.

Perhaps it is because I am one who constantly works with extrasensory faculties that I dwell on this matter of believing that there are no insurmountable barriers between us and the answer to our need. There is something about disbelief that blocks the reach of the mind. This has been demonstrated to me many times. For instance, someone comes to me for a sitting but just before I go into trance he explains that he does not believe it is possible for the dead to communicate with the living; he says the whole idea is contrary to sense. When I see his negative attitude I know in advance that he will probably not have a good sitting. The chances are that Fletcher may be very short with him, possibly through sheer inability to get him in focus. It has been suggested that disbelief sets up a negative current which counteracts the vital force that seems in some way to encompass us all in a field of energy during a trance session. Or perhaps Fletcher finds that persons on his side feel there is no use trying to reach the sitter. Perhaps also at some deep level my mind is saying, "It can't be done; it can't be done." Whatever the combination of reasons, I have found that unfaith is a practical barrier to communication.

People who do spiritual healing have also told me that faith seems to be a prerequisite for healing, except in the case of children for whom someone else's faith seems to suffice. Likewise persons directing a large-scale testing program, in which symbols on cards are supposed to be read before the cards are exposed, have found that those who do not believe clairvoyance is possible average a lower score than those who do believe. If faith operates in these concrete situations it seems reasonable that it also operates in the matter of getting a solution to our complex problems. Faith is essential in the operation of parapsychological faculties.

As soon as we begin to pray with faith, believing that our needs will be met in supernormal ways if necessary, then we are bound to be struck by the persistence and ingenuity with which the answers come. Sometimes our prayer is no sooner articulated than the answer floods in. This is especially true when a matter of motivation or attitude is concerned; in a flash that amounts to revelation we may see our relationship to our problem in its true light and at the instant of seeing, our attitude changes! But sometimes the answer is not so immediate. We may leave our place of prayer with the same problem we brought in but our feeling toward it has changed; we have a feeling of expectancy because we know that the answer is coming. And in a matter of hours, or perhaps of days, someone comes to us, or some situation occurs which suggests the solution. It seems evident that there is definite planning in the ways the anwers are brought to our attention. We would almost say that the answers are seeking us; indeed, they sometimes seem to have been on their way before our problem was stated. "Before you call I will answer."

This process of asking and receiving may go on for quite some time before we are one day aware that a tremendous change has taken place in our ideas about God. He is no longer an impersonal power. We realize that only someone who cares about us could so personally supervise our well-being. We are loved! Our God is mindful of us. If we stumble, instantly we feel his steadying hand. If we exceed our usual modest generosity or perform a kindness beyond our custom, we all but see his nod of approval. Here is companionship beyond anything we have known before. We have become friends with God. This is a non-theological statement of a tremendous fact.

Some people speak of going apart to pray as "going into the Presence," and this is a good phrase for while God is not more present in one place than another, he is only present for us when we turn our attention to him. A day comes when, as we go into the Presence, we feel him so close, so real, that we stand amazed. How could this be! God! Our heart overflows. We have no words for what we feel. Maybe words of the psalmist rush forth and we speak them because we have to express something. Or we may break into a hymn. However we respond we are experiencing the prayer of thanksgiving. Moreover, once we have experienced it, the mood of praise will come easily upon us. Our gratitude that God *is,* and is available, and is love, will motivate our life.

If we have a stated time of prayer, perhaps a half-hour at the beginning of the day, we may sometimes find that the whole period has been devoted to sheer adoration. There may be no time left for considering whatever problem we had planned to present to God. Nevertheless it will be answered in the usual way. It was our attention which needed focusing on him, not his on us. The answer to our need is inherent in his presence.

Sometimes when we are absorbed in praise and thanksgiving we may find ourself lost in consideration of some particular quality which God personifies. His kindness, say; or his justice. His mercy, his truth, his reliability. His love! We ponder in terms of the incidents in which he has dealt with us. And then we ponder upon his nature. As we feel ourself drawn toward him we may lose ourself in our meditation until we have no sense of self at all.

All meditation is not spontaneous, however. We may deliberately plan an exercise in meditation upon some aspect of the nature of God. We have to choose some facet or factor of his being with which we have had intimate experience. These exercises are necessary if we ever expect God to do his perfect work in us. This too is a method of attending and of trying to become one with the object of our thought. And like all exercises in concentration, meditation upon the nature of God needs to be done regularly. In time we only need to initiate the meditation and we will find ourself swept into it. In time also meditation may become so all-absorbing that the mind loses contact with the outer world, the body is stilled in a trancelike sleep, and only the soul is alert. This too is prayer.

Some people find it difficult to meditate on an aspect of God. Not being able to visualize him, he does not seem quite real. But they can visualize his expression in Jesus. They know Jesus in terms of concrete incidents in his life, and to him they respond. They can tell him their troubles and toward him their gratitude is readily expressed. For them meditating on some incident in his life is more meaningful than trying to meditate on God. Such meditation may also have great value. I have found it so.

We may decide to try to enter into the life of Jesus as recorded in the Scriptures, so far as it is possible. To make the experience vivid we need to be a participant in each incident. Perhaps we are an unknown disciple; or one of those whom he healed and who perhaps afterward stayed as near as possible to him. Perhaps we are a member of his family or a neighbor. We may begin by meditating on his birth. What was the reaction of the others around him—

his parents, his kinfolk; the shepherds, the wisemen, the king; the neighbors; the elders in the synagogue?

We may go on to meditate on his visit to Jerusalem at twelve years. Perhaps we now appraise him through the eyes of one of the priests whom he consulted. What seems to be the home background of this boy who asks such persistent and intelligent questions? And what are his questions? What do we say when he asks our opinion on the coming of the Messiah? What does he say when we ask what he thinks will be the marks of the Messiah? Why does he ask if the Messiah will know even as a boy that he is indeed the Messiah? Although we begin our meditation trying to see Jesus the boy through the eyes of one of the priests he interrogated, we are almost sure to be drawn into the mind of the boy himself. And to the measure that we are drawn in, the incident yields its meaning.

Many have used this kind of meditation to bring themselves, for love of Christ, under his direction. When we thus enter into his life then his teaching seems inevitable and his miracles no longer strange. If we can vividly participate in a healing miracle while in this kind of meditation, it is very likely that we will feel healing power rise in us. We will feel an impulsion to heal. And we will heal. That is, the power will work through us to heal. It is the nature of true meditation that our consciousness will be expanded in the direction in which expansion is needed— in this case, healing. This is a fact which no one can either deny or affirm until he has meditated consistently for a long time.

Besides the prayer which is a cry of help for ourself, and the prayer of thanksgiving and praise, and the prayer of meditation and contemplation, there remains intercessory prayer. There are always others whose needs become as our own. This is true, of course, from the time of our first desperate need of help, for most of our own problems involve someone else and we cannot find our own relationship to our troubles without also becoming aware of other people's relationship to us. As we go on in prayer our awareness expands and we become increasingly conscious of the needs of those around us. It is then as natural to pray for others as for ourself.

To pray for another means to try to stand in his stead before God. This is only possible by means of concentrated awareness of the other person. Merely to say the words "God bless my neighbor" is no use unless we can be acutely conscious of our neighbor. A prayer in which empathy is lacking between the one who prays and the one prayed for cannot register with that power which answers. This is not a case of a temperamental God's refusing to answer, but a matter of law. One of the laws of prayer is attention, concentration. We have to attend to our neighbor in the sense of becoming one with him. This is the same process at work in psychometry; it is a oneing process. When separateness is obliterated, then I can indeed pray for him.

Attention being a psychophysical process demanding energy, we cannot attend intensively to many interests in sequence. Hence it is difficult to pray for many persons with a sense of their individual needs. We can pray only so long as we can attend. Thus periods of intercessory prayer usually have to be short, and they seem most effective after meditation when attention has been brought to its keenest pitch. People who do spiritual healing know these same limitations of attention. The healing power wells up, is passed on to a few individuals, then it seems to die down and lie latent for a time before it gathers together and wells up again. A similar law seems to be at work in healing and in intercessory prayer.

One of the most effective forms of intercessory prayer is

to take the one in need with us, mentally, when we go into the Presence to meditate. Then although our attention shifts from the one in need to God himself, the one for whom we are praying shares in the transforming power of God's presence. His need is met as surely as if the time had been spent in petition.

There is another way we can help link someone in need with the power of God. At a time when the individual's attention is not directed elsewhere, preferably when he is asleep, we can silently call him by name, repeating his name steadily until we feel as if his attention is aroused, and then we can remind him affirmatively that God is equal to his need. God is available to him; God is at hand; God has the resources, the wisdom, the love, the power. He has only to ask in longing; he needs only to turn for help in honest determination to accept it on its own terms. But when thus addressing another we need to take particular care that no self-interest is involved. If the core of the mind which receives such communication has any feeling that we are manipulating the individual for our own ends, it will not co-operate in bringing our prayer to his waking attention. We have to communicate with the conviction born of experience; there must be authority in what we say. This is a method of prayer I have used countless times with transforming results. Its method is telepathy but it is much more than an exercise in telepathy.

Out of long experience in intercessory prayer we come to know that the lives which touch ours are indeed bound together with us. At some deep level our needs are one and communication is possible to those who will to communicate. When there is a common dedication of purpose then the flow of minds may become a tremendous factor in bringing the power of God to bear upon a common aim. Jesus must have had this fact in mind when he said that where two or three were gathered together in his name there he was in their midst. It is this pooling of intent which makes a prayer group powerful in intercession. It also makes a greatly enhanced inspiration possible.

I am convinced that much that we call inspiration is really co-operation between like minds willing to share both ideas and energy. The joint effort is telepathic but it has to be with intent to further a common end, even though the intention does not reach the threshold of consciousness. This is the way great reform movements are started, gather impetus, and accomplish the seemingly impossible. This is the way spiritual revivals may sweep the land. This is the way of accomplishing God's larger purposes.

Moreover, this pooling of effort and aspiration may include both incarnate and discarnate persons. Handel reported that after a long period in which he had produced nothing he had great longing to compose again. He sat for three days and nights, he says, motionless and listening, gazing into heaven, not conscious of people around him nor of the food they brought. Then suddenly he knew that he was hearing music inaudible to other ears. Transfixed he listened inwardly. And then he seized pen and paper and wrote out *The Messiah*. In the light of my own experience I can only wonder if the triumphant mood of the Hallelujah Chorus may not have been induced in part by the triumphant sense of achievement on the part of invisible musicians who beamed in the music he insists he heard in his mind.

George Washington Carver, a chemist whose work on the peanut alone made agricultural and industrial history for the South, often described his method of invention as one of request and listening. "*Then* the thing I am about to do and the way of doing come to me. I never have to grope for methods. The method is revealed at the moment and I am inspired to create something new. Without God to draw aside the curtain I would be helpless." Again he commented, "My prayers are more an attitude than anything else. But I ask the Great Creator silently and daily, and often many times a day, to permit me to speak to him through the three great kingdoms of the world which he has created—the animal, mineral and vegetable kingdoms—to understand their relations to each other and our relations to them, and to the great God who made all of us. I ask him daily and often momently to give me wisdom, understanding and bodily strength to do his will; hence I am asking and receiving all the time."

Could it not be that unseen colleagues were working with him, both to augment his intent and to answer his prayer? God is not less present because his process in answering prayer utilizes laws of which we are now beginning to be aware. Prayer takes on new dimensions and new urgency when seen in the context of the higher laws at work—many of them apparently the laws of the paranormal. A Carver prays as he psychometrizes a peanut and the secrets it yields become the answer to the prayers of tens of thousands of hungry people. A clairaudient Handel becomes the liaison composer translating the celestial harmony of invisible musicians for the sake of the heart-hunger of thousands who are lifted nearer God by their joint creation.

It seems to me apparent that prayer is a direct transaction between man and God, but it also seems apparent that often God answers each of us by way of some of the rest of us.

One day when I was in trance a woman asked help for a friend of hers. I am told that a former doctor responded, "Your friend will have to do her own asking."

"She doesn't know how," the woman remonstrated, "and she needs help."

The answer was, "Just let her lay her heart open and express her deep desire to the Most High, who knows it already. Let her ask believing. Let her ask in faith, knowing that his ear is never closed. Then someone in heaven or earth will get the answer to her. This is the law. But every man has to do his own asking, seeking, knocking. And at the same time he has to be willing to be used to answer the seeking of others."

Perhaps the development of psychic faculties on the part of those who pray is a necessary step in the evolution of awareness of the oneness of all who turn to God, whether on this earth or in the invisible realm.

CHAPTER 20

A New Frontier

I AM CONVINCED that those theologians and ministers who discount the miracles recorded in the New Testament do so because they cannot believe in the suspension of natural law; and knowing nothing of the laws which operate in the extrasensory aspects of our universe, they are forced to devise an explanation in accord with their limited epistemology. They cannot conceive of the record of the early church as factual because, to their minds, such things do not, and can not happen.

It always appalls me when theologians are less open to new facts than biologists, and when psychologists are more dogmatic—more under the spell of positivism—than the physical scientists. The reason I am dismayed is because ministers seem to have a better speaking acquaintance with theology and psychology than with other disciplines, and yet they are the ones who constantly have to deal with a Scripture which documents the very psychic phenomena they cannot accommodate to their thinking, and with the living experience of prayer which induces psychic phenomena.

At first glance it seems strange that a culture such as ours which has developed so many fields of inquiry should not have included the field of psychic research. But science, which dominates our culture, has progressed by means of experiments which were capable of repetition and proof. And admittedly psychic phenomena are not always amenable to proof by repeated experiment. Some experiments do arrive twice, or a dozen times, at the same results but as often as not conditions which seem identical produce divergent results or none at all. Thus by standards of scientific inquiry psychic findings are declared to be subjective, or by some other semantic device relegated outside the pale of serious consideration. However, scientists themselves are beginning to acknowledge that in many cases the experimenter is a factor in the experiment. Certainly a psychically endowed individual knows himself to be both experimenter and apparatus.

When it comes to appraising psychic matters most ministers, caught in their culture but free in their experience, have been confronted by a difficult choice: either they have had to take a stand for the reality of psychic experience—which could not occur if the basic structure of the only science they knew was correctly conceived—or they had to insist that there was something the matter with the structure of scientific thought because it could not accommodate parapsychological experience. Either stance seemed presumptuous.

Nevertheless, psychic data have continued to pile up and, with the increasing popularity of prayer groups in churches, are being brought forcibly to the attention of an increasing number of ministers. It is time that the gap between the terra firma of sensory experience and the terra incognita of extrasensory experience be bridged. And it looks as if the physicists and biologists have at last thrown a rope across. Physics and biology are not my fields, nor are they the special interests of most ministers, but I note that many are reading with excitement some of the reports of both groups. It cannot help astounding some ministers to find the astro-physicists who once felt their feet to be upon the solidest of ground now acknowledging that they are not only swinging on a star but that the light given off by the star consists of both waves and particles, contradictory conceptions both of which seem borne out by experiment. Further, such an outstanding atomic scientist as Robert Oppenheimer comments on the hazardous position of scientists who deal with the smallest known charges of energy.

To what appeared to be the simplest questions we will tend to give either no answer or an answer which will at first sight be reminiscent more of a strange catechism than of the straight-forward affirmations of physical science. If we ask, for instance, whether the position of the electron remains the same, we must say 'no'; if we ask whether the electron's position changes with time, we must say 'no'; if we ask whether the electron is at rest, we must say 'no'; if we ask whether it is in motion, we must say 'no'. The Buddha has given such answers when interrogated as to the condition of man's self after death; but they are not familiar answers for the tradition of seventeenth- and eighteenth-century science.

Maybe such observations do not prove that the physicist and the parapsychologist are standing on the same platform somewhere in outer space but they do suggest that incon-clusiveness is no longer a mark of warped observation. And perhaps ordinary persons who have psychic endowment can help to weave a cable of fact which can be used to sup-port a bridge across the chasm which now separates the theologians and the parapsychologists.

In my earlier day I often noted that ministers who saw the relevance of psychic phenomena to their task often felt conspicuous as news of their interests spread around among their brethren. But I also noted that the interested ones had a way of finding each other out. In the late twenties, in England, Rev. G. Maurice Elliott and St. Clair Stobart decided it was time to get those interested into some kind of loose organization so that they could exchange ideas, books, monographs, and reports, and also at times meet together. Thus an organization known as the Confraternity came into being. The group grew steadily and a good many distinguished names were added.

After Mrs. Stobart's death the Confraternity languished a bit until following World War II, Maurice Elliott and Lt. Col. Reginald M. Lester, a journalist, revived the interest and organized the Churches Fellowship for Psychic Studies. The group now numbers twenty-three hundred members, among them such dignitaries as the Bishop of Ripon, the Bishop of Sheffield, the Bishop of Worcester, the Dean of St. Paul's, and Dr. Leslie Weatherhead of the City Temple, London. Their magazine serves as both house organ and a forum for exchange of thought. It seemed to me on a recent visit to England that the climate had changed in many churches. Both general and scholarly attention is turned toward the relationship of extrasensory experience to religion.

With the British organization in mind I used often to wish that American clergymen had a comparable clearing house. In the winter of 1956 when I was in Chicago I talked with Paul Higgins and the late Albin Bro about the possibility of calling together in an informal fashion such clergymen and interested friends as might care to meet over a weekend to pool their interest and findings in the three related fields of prayer, spiritual healing and survival. Mrs. Victor Munnecke joined them to form a planning committee and they sent out about fifty inquiries and set a tentative date. Almost immediately letters and telegrams began to arrive from various parts of the country; others wished to be included. And thus the contemplated seminar grew into a sizable meeting which was held in the Hyde Park Methodist Church, Chicago.

The program was comprehensive, the discussion animated, and the interest vigorous enough so that a permanent organization was formed, called Spiritual Frontiers Fellowship. Paul Higgins became the first president and Edmond Dyett the executive secretary. A monthly publication keeps the members in touch with one another and regional gatherings have brought new members so that now the new organization numbers around six hundred. A research program and many study groups are flourishing.

Certainly experience such as mine raises questions with which religious people, such as those meeting in these groups, will have to deal. For instance, any one who sits in on a considerable number of trance sessions will accumulate a good deal of evidence that personality persists after death. But whether it actually persists as an organization of individual traits having a self-directed life or whether it persists only as a well-defined record, which in some way is available to the medium, is more difficult to determine.

The case for a permanent record somehow imposed upon time-space has been attested by psychics at least since early Egyptian and Indian days. To be sure, the only "fact" offered in proof of such a record is the ability of trained seers, without collusion, to concentrate upon a given individual and read back much the same story of past experience, both from his current lifetime and from hypothetical previous lifetimes. No doubt there are such trained seers alive today, but they are less likely to be found in our western culture, which affords small training along such lines, than in an eastern culture which guards and fosters such gifts. Such persons could, of course, be sought out and with their co-operation some significant findings might be brought to light. The question is what such an individual is experiencing—a break-through of memory from a previous lifetime? Or imagining a scene of remarkable authenticity as to details to which he is not likely to have had access in this life? Or catching a glimpse of recorded phenomena? In the latter case one has to presuppose a continuum of waves and particles of light and of sound waves—and perhaps of some other kind of waves—which are discernible to some built-in receiving apparatus peculiar to humankind.

That some sort of permanent record does exist has been, and is, attested by a sufficient number of persons to make the hypothesis worthy of study. If instead of being called the akashic record, meaning space, ether or sky, as the Hindu tradition conceives the continuum to be, this permanent registry were given a new name in keeping with the latest development of modern physics, experimentation might proceed more briskly and with less apology.

Another question: if from the akashic record a psychic is reading back the history of John Brown's deceased grandfather, let us say, and merely predicating the continued existence of the grandfather, then the psychic's motivation has to be established. Why would I, or any other psychic, utilize the elaborate device of personalizing the record as being the grandfather? Simply because the desire of the client—and of millions of clients of other mediums before me—persuades me to the device at some subconscious level? But there is also the predicated grandfather's discriminating use of the past and present tense to account for. And his prognostications of the future. Do I in trance glimpse the record before it is made—so far as our ordinary conceptions of time-space are concerned? This possibility would not seem too strange to modern physics.

Moreover, granted that a medium may be in touch with the persisting personality of John Brown's grandfather, can John Brown therefore deduce that the personality of his grandfather will continue to exist through all time? An affirmative answer is not deducible from any evidence I have seen—although I believe that something of the kind is a fact.

It interests me that great-great grandfathers do not appear in my seances. Historical figures do not appear. Now if a physicist is having a sitting for the purpose of acquiring information from discarnate colleagues on a given problem, why do not Faraday or Davy, Oersted or Ampère manifest themselves? Certainly not for lack of interest if the client is a scientist of their own caliber.

Here the only noteworthy comment comes from the discarnates themselves. For what it is worth, their explanation is that in communication between the incarnate and the discarnate we are involved in a problem in transfer of energy. Each individual, as a combination of energies in fluctuating pattern, influences every other individual who shares the same field of force. Indeed, a certain quantum of energy is constantly exchanged between individuals. Put it that individual A and individual X exchange a definite charge of energy, the amount varying according to the intensity and frequency of the contact. This exchange of energy effects a permanent channel of communication. The channel having once been opened, interchange is possible between those two individuals—given an impetus of need and acquiescence—whether both are living, one of them discarnate, or both discarnate. Moreover, a third individual, K, who has had contact with both A and X at some time, can relay conversation from one to the other, but he cannot put A and X in direct contact.

With any individual this criss-crossing of "wires" of

energy binds him to many persons, perhaps to thousands of persons. Many of them continue to live with him in the context of daily life as he knows it in the physical body; as the years go by an increasing number of them move into the discarnate state. But the ties persist. If John Brown, living, once touched his great-grandfather, they remain in touch; the possibility of direct communication persists. If John Brown never knew his great-grandfather, then the best he can do is to get someone like his grandfather, who knows them both, to transmit communication. And even that is only possible if both John Brown and his great-grandfather desire this indirect communication.

There are also questions to be asked as to where the psychic and the creative processes impinge upon each other. May the creative process—say literary invention— actually be a dual endeavor compounded of one mind's desire to invent a character, or a set of characters within the framework of a plot, and some answering mind's throwing back of an actual character or plot lifted from the akashic record? A helpful hint is furnished by the way in which characters take over their author and insist upon their own action. Are the creative artists in the fields of music, painting, drama, poetry and the like more open to psychic experience than those who do not exercise their creative faculties? What about inventors in general? Where does an individual's part in the creative process leave off and a co-operative venture begin? A careful reading of the autobiographies of creative personalities poses some interesting possibilities.

There are other possible reasons why a medium does not bring to the fore personalities from the more remote past. But here again the information comes through psychics or from discarnates and has only such theoretical value as accrues to any coherent structure of thought.

Discarnate personalities may, in the process of maturation, move on into another dimension of consciousness expressed in a finer energy pattern, in which state they may be concerned with other than earth problems. Apparently all degrees of consciousness are amenable to direction from higher forms of consciousness, subject—at least in part—to the censure of their own free will. Thus these advanced personalities may or may not be on call when John Brown addresses them by name. However, John Brown's call does not go unanswered. It appears to be a law of the universe that one who seeks, knocks, calls, is answered.

The *modus operandi* of the spiritual universe may not be as simple as has been delineated by some systems of religious thought but the fact appears to stand that no one who needs help is ever ignored, unheard, or slighted. Nor does an answer depend upon the caprice of any person, incarnate or discarnate. If John Brown, in an agony of longing for strength to follow a difficult course, calls upon his discarnate grandfather who was known for his courage and the grandfather should refuse to answer, then someone else takes the call and answers. "This is the way the universe is set up," remarked a philosophic discarnate. "It is the law and it operates with the precision of law. The humblest of hearts may call upon the Almighty and in a sense the call is a command, for God has chosen to operate through this law that prayers are heard and answered. The chain of command may at times be intricate but it is instantaneous and sure."

I expect to see the ministers move in on more of these concerns. After all, the church was born in a psychic experience on the day of Pentecost. Moreover, I have seen the life of a minister—and also his sermons and the size of his congregation—changed by his own experience with psychic phenomena. The first minister I knew well whose point of view was changed by his own psychic experience was named Arthur Ford! He was shaken to the boots and in the process his cosmology, epistemology, theology and all his other *ologies* had to be reconstituted. Then I saw the preaching of Alonzo Fortune take on a new authority as he quietly went about substantiating the psychic aspects of the gospel record.

My next major contact with a minister to whom the psychic reports of the Bible became a continued story was with Robert Norwood. I remember his telling about his experiences at Holy Communion. Having myself grown up in a denomination which makes the Lord's Supper central in the Sunday morning worship service, I was touched to find this great man in a liturgical setting experiencing the "goodly company" of the departed gathering with those at the table. He told me that as men and women knelt at the altar rail he often saw those dear to them, supposedly dead, standing behind them or kneeling beside them; he saw a father slip an arm across a son's shoulder, a mother take her daughter's hand, a child slip in between parents. Sometimes an unseen loved one would quietly tell him the hidden problem of the one whom he was serving and he would find his own prayers winged with new longing for this needy child of God.

Emmet Fox was a minister who took the New Testament record at its face value. It was while I was on my second visit to London, living in Horace Leaf's house, that he first came to see me. Before that time I had never heard of him and he told me nothing about his metaphysical interests until after the sitting. But through Fletcher some of his own people, discarnates, came to him that day and urged him to accept an invitation he had just received to take over a group in New York City. Fox was much amazed that his unseen friends knew of his offer and decided to accept the invitation. During the years when he was speaking to his enormous audiences in New York we met often; as a matter of fact we lived in the same hotel for two years and had many discussions both of his work and my own. He expected anyone who accepted the metaphysical system which he taught—which he always felt was simply the metaphysics of Jesus—to take for granted the survival of personality and the flow of communication between the living and the dead.

Whenever I think of ministers who have come up against the psyshic with something of a sense of shock, an Anglican clergyman named Winekoop comes to my mind. I met him at the Lyceum Club which was a club of professional women writers in England. Mrs. de Crespigny was a member and it was she who persuaded me to lecture there. Naturally I expected an all-woman audience, which was challenge enough for any speaker because these intelligent British women delighted to heckle. However, there was this one man present. At the time I did not know he was a convinced disbeliever in things psychic. During the period after the lecture when I was giving messages from whatever discarnates manifested themselves clairvoyantly, a message came for this clergyman. After the meeting I could see that he was shaken, so I took him along with me to join a group at Conan Doyle's home and that occasion proved the beginning of his interest in the investigation of psychic phenomena. A year or so later when I returned to London he told me that he had recently summoned courage to tell his congregation, in a church on Finchley Road, that he was convinced of survival and communication. He said that when he went into his pulpit he had his resignation in his pocket, feeling sure he would be asked for it at the end of the service. Since this was to be his last sermon he told them all the things he felt they ought to know in support of the New Testament claim of everlasting life. After the service he waited bravely for remonstrances to overwhelm him. "You can imagine my astonishment," he said to me, "when the congregation surged up to congratulate me on having caught up with them at last."

Another British clergyman high in my regard was the Scotsman John Lamond, earlier the pastor of Greensides Church, Edinburgh. After World War I he began to receive messages from his daughter Kathleen, a nurse who had died in France in World War I. When he became convinced of survival he publicly stated his position, and the result was that he had to leave his church. Thereafter he spoke all over the United Kingdom. He was a big man both physically and spiritually. I have often shared the platform with him and was unfailingly stirred by the depth of his perception. After Conan Doyle's death a number of prominent men of letters wanted to write Doyle's life story, but Lady Doyle could never bring herself to decide who should be the official biographer. Then one day when Dr. Lamond was having a sitting with me, Doyle came through with the pronouncement that he wanted to have him write the biography, promising to help as needed. Lady Doyle felt that the message from her husband was genuine and commissioned Lamond to proceed. Thereafter for a period of several months Lamond came to me regularly with his manuscript and in my trance Sir Arthur corrected and added details. Obviously I was not conscious of the page-by-page work but in his preface to the book Dr. Lamond states that the book could not have been written without "the constant co-operation of Arthur Ford."

Back in the thirties, as one result of the growing interest of the clergy in psychic affairs, Cosmo Lang, Archbishop of Canterbury, appointed a committee to inquire into the claims of spiritualism. During one of my visits to London,

St. Clair Stobart invited this committee and several other clergymen to meet me at tea. After I had finished conveying messages from such invisible friends of theirs as put in their long-distance calls, an animated—and indeed heated—discussion was soon in full flame. At one point a priest of the Anglo-Catholic persuasion began his comments with the phrase, "In the hour of the Holy Mass . . . ," whereupon a low churchman responded, "You mean during Communion . . . " and someone else interjected, "He means during the Lord's Supper." Then the oldest and probably the most distinguished of them all—I learned afterward that he was the Canon of Christ Church, Westminster—stood up and settled the argument by saying, "Holy mass, holy communion, HOLY MACKEREL!" This induced silence by shock. The Canon then went on to say, "We have been arguing this subject for two hundred years. Today we came to hear about something of significance which we have previously overlooked. So let us confine our remarks to the subject."

Later this committee of the Archbishop's turned in a favorable report on the findings of Spiritualism but the Archbishop pigeonholed the report and it was only after widespread demand, led by Hannen Swaffer, that it was made public.

Dr. Ozora Davis, once moderator of the Congregational Churches in the United States and also president of the Chicago Theological Seminary, was one of the forward-looking ministers who felt that modern physics would one day come to the support of a psychology of the paranormal. In one of his last speeches he said, "There will be no Protestant church in America in fifty years unless we accept and use the findings of psychical research." He had many sittings with me; indeed, I sat for him and members of his family and a few of his faculty friends the night before he left for his last trip to California—the trip on which he died.

Dr. William H. Leach, editor of *Church Management*, has taken a good many occasions to pass on the light he feels he has received through Fletcher. Like others of my friends he sometimes tells me what goes on in my trance. He had a sitting shortly after the death of his brother Earl who was ten years his senior. The brother had been confined to his bed for several years, crippled with paralysis. On this day Fletcher reported his brother as remarking, "I hardly know what to say yet. I've been here such a short time that I'm not as yet oriented. In fact I was surprised to find myself here. I have seen Mother and Father. I hardly knew Mother; she looked so young. This is one thing which will interest you—here we project the age we wish to be. Hot dog! You should see me. I'm just twenty-five years old."

Leach felt it was the kind of remark his brother would make if he had taken any other kind of trip to an unknown country and Leach had called him on the long-distance phone. Some way I have always preferred this human little story to many more involved and evidential reports that have come back to me through Leach.

Sometimes it costs ministers something to come out firmly in behalf of their convictions in regard to psychic phenomena. Dr. Davis spoke his mind in a day before the interest of the universities in parapsychology had made such concerns respectable. In that connection I always think of old John Hill, pastor of a one-room Spiritualist church in a poor section of New York City back in the days when law classified mediumship with fortunetelling. Finally a new law was passed in New York and thereafter authenticated ministers under jurisdiction of the General Assembly of Spiritualist Churches could not be arrested. But many times in the old days I have gone to the Fifty-seventh Street jail to advance the five-hundred-dollars' bail required for release of a medium.

John Hill was a man of single-minded devotion to his beliefs; if life was everlasting, just as the Good Book held, then he intended that people receive proof of the fact through his mediumship. On one occasion he was taken before a magistrate who offered to let him go if he would "quit pretending to communicate" but if he did not give his promise he would have to go to jail for three months. That word "pretending" was too much for John. He drew himself up and said that if Peter, James and John could accept prison in preference to ceasing to speak their gospel, so could he. So he served out his time on Welfare Island. His witness was not without repercussions; Ethel Corbin, then one of the oldest policewomen on the force, was converted from listening to John's testimony.

Ernest Holmes is another man who has always stanchly expressed his convictions. Periodically for years he has had sittings with me and I count him one of the most discerning men I know. His enormous following is left in no doubt as to his point of view and he uses his magazine, *Science of Mind*, as a means of bringing the findings of some of the most distinguished men of modern science to bear on the revelations of the psychic.

Dr. Lewis L. Dunnington, pastor of the First Methodist Church of Iowa City, Iowa, is another minister who speaks out in his pulpit for the modern duplication of the psychic phenomena of the early Church. I heard him speak twice on a Sunday morning to his great church full of people on his belief in ongoing life and communication, making use of firsthand illustrations from his own experience. That evening a group of his friends and fellow ministers, including Dr. Marcus Bach, gathered for a seance. I have also lectured and demonstrated platform clairvoyance in his church.

Increasingly churches are discovering the inevitability of psychic experience in disciplined devotion. A change in the character of prayer groups is notable. Silent meditation is almost customary and this kind of heightened attention is likely to produce some awareness of unseen presences as well as to quicken spiritual healing.

Rev. Paul L. Higgins, pastor of the Hyde Park Methodist Church of Chicago, first began to be aware of discarnate presences in a prayer group which met weekly to pray for the sick. He made his experiences known to some members of his official church board and their interest led to their investigation of the psychic field. Later he invited me to meet with a group of his members for a seance in the prayer room of his church. Still later several open meetings were held in which the seance became a kind of testimonial to the life of the church invisible.

Glenn Clark was another who constantly felt the aid of those he loved who had disappeared from his earthly sight. I remember that the first time he came to me for a sitting he was almost apologetic that he should need a go-between to converse with the invisible members of his family. Actually I think he did not need one for he had his own method of communication. Some of his followers were shocked that he should seek out a medium; in fact, one of the group who accompanied him told me later that she would never have come near me if anyone but Glenn Clark had suggested it. That woman is now a very good medium herself. Not many months before he died Glenn Clark expressed the feeling that so many former members of his prayer groups had gone on to their heavenly home where their vistas were wider and their power greater that his Camps Farthest Out were able to take on tasks they could never have carried when all of their members were earthbound. He also felt that his own going would push their horizons still further out—and such indeed seems to be the case.

There is a quality about meetings in which unseen

presences are manifest. On Easter Eve, 1957, I met with a group of fifteen ministers of old-line Protestant churches in a suburb of Philadelphia; they were joined by many invisible colleagues and friends. I am told that some of the Easter sermons preached that next morning had an authority new to the congregation.

Easter evening my friend Melvin Sutley gathered another group of ministers and friends for the same kind of evening. From there I went to Cleveland to meet for two evenings with a larger group of ministers and friends to discuss the place of communication in the gamut of spiritual gifts listed by St. Paul, and to allow discarnate friends to contribute to the colloquy. The men in these groups, it became evident to me in the discussion period, were not without psychic experience of their own.

Many ministers have become interested in parapsychology, I note, because they have had psychic experiences of their own. Sometimes they wonder if they should have had them. They are at times astounded that when they have prayed for the sick, upon request, the sick were healed. One minister mentioned to me recently that it should be surprising if men who spend so much of their time encouraging the sick, assuring the dying of eternal life, comforting the bereaved, did not look for veridical evidence of spiritual healing, survival and communication, and answered prayer. I have noticed for some time that the men who make their firsthand testimony of experience in these lines are the men who fill their churches.

In recent months I have met with groups in a variety of churches, including Broadway Tabernacle, a Congregational church in New York of which Rev. Albert Penner is the pastor; in St. Peter's Episcopalian Church, in Chicago; in the First Methodist Church of La Grange, of which Rev. Lester Minion is the minister; in the Burnside Methodist

Church of East Hartford, Connecticut, of which Rev. Ralph Henard was then the minister; with the Ministerial Association of South Bend, Indiana, and so on. To call the roll is only to italicize the growing interest of ministers. In the Chicago meetings I have noted the presence of seminary students; in a recent meeting in Trenton, New Jersey, both the students and faculty of Princeton Theological Seminary were represented.

And at all these meetings there are present and speaking some ministers not visible to the eye but eager to add their testimony through Fletcher. Indeed a list of the former dignitaries of many denominations and of the faithful ministers of many churches who have spoken through Fletcher might surprise those who think of them as having served their term and gone on. They are often still serving, both as friends of their former parishioners and in their own pulpits, as unseen support of the present preacher.

Some discarnate ministers speak of having churches of their own in their present situation. "Once a minister always a minister," remarked one fine old gentleman. "Don't you think that we gather for worship in our aspect of the universe? And don't you think we enjoy hearing a good sermon *and* preaching a good sermon? Here we don't have to try to convince anybody that life goes on, although you might be surprised to know that there are those here among us who simply do not believe in what Paul called 'the third heaven.' Well, it is real, all right, and there are spirits from that estate who communicate with us and lend us their aid just as we try to co-operate with you. God is immanent in his whole creation and it is a lot more complex than you or we have yet taken in."

I wonder if the interest of these new-old frontiers may not bring back into the churches some of the thousands of members who have been lost to the cults and esoteric movements which for the past half century have taken over the psychic aspects of religion. Survival is not the only tenet of the gospel but it is the one without which the others lose much of their significance. One has only to see the transformation in the lives of some who suddenly realize that personality is not lost in death to know how basic this assurance is. Likewise one has only to experience the cooperation of unseen presences still animated by love and dedicated to service to know that the company of the righteous is invincible.

Paul understood this working together for the common good: "Now there are varieties of gifts, but the same Spirit; and there are varieties of service, but the same Lord; and there are varieties of working, but it is the same God who inspires them all in every one." Then after naming over the psychic gifts and exhorting his listeners earnestly to desire these higher gifts, he puts them all into proper relationship with a final admonition, "Make love your aim."

And this I take to be the aim of expanded consciousness—the full awareness and perfect expression of love.

Index